by ROBERT KELLY

Armed Descent (1961)
Her Body Against Time
  (1963)
Round Dances (1964)
Enstasy (1964)
Lunes (1964)
Lectiones (1965)
Words in Service (1965)
Weeks (1966)
The Scorpions (1967)
Song XXIV (1967)
Devotions (1967)
Twenty Poems (1967)
Axon Dendron Tree (1967)
Crooked Bridge Love Society
  (1967)
A Joining (1967)
Alpha (1968)
Finding the Measure (1968)
Sonnets (1968)
Statement (1968)
Songs I–XXX (1968)
The Common Shore (1969)
A California Journal (1969)
Kali Yuga (1970)
Cities (1971)
In Time (1971)
Flesh Dream Book (1971)
Ralegh (1972)
The Pastorals (1972)
Reading Her Notes (1972)

The Tears of Edmund Burke
  (1973)
The Mill of Particulars (1973)
A Line of Sight (1974)
The Loom (1975)
Sixteen Odes (1976)
The Lady Of (1977)
The Convections (1978)
Wheres (1978)
The Book of Persephone (1978)
The Cruise of the Pnyx (1979)
Kill the Messenger Who Brings
  Bad News (1979)
Sentence (1980)
Spiritual Exercises (1981)
The Alchemist to Mercury
  (1981)
Mulberry Women (1982)
Under Words (1983)
Thor's Thrush (1984)
A Transparent Tree (1985)
The Scorpions (new edition,
  1985)
Not This Island Music (1987)
Doctor of Silence (1988)
Oahu (1988)
Cat Scratch Fever (1990)
Ariadne (1991)
A Strange Market (1992) .
Red Actions: Selected Poems
  1960–1993 (1995)

Editor
A Controversy of Poets (1965)

ROBERT KELLY

RED ACTIONS

SELECTED POEMS 1960-1993

BLACK SPARROW PRESS
SANTA ROSA · 1995

ACKNOWLEDGMENTS

Most of the compositions in the group "Poems from 1991–1993" have appeared in magazines: *Conjunctions* (Bradford Morrow), *Grand Street* (Jean Stein and Erik Reiselbach), *Notus* (Pat and Marla Smith), *Bombay Gin* (Cindy Dach and Anne Waldman). "Set on War" was first published in Edward Sanders' *Anthology of Gulf War Poems.*

LIBRARY OF CONGRESS CATALOGING-IN-PUBLICATION DATA

Kelly, Robert, 1935–
    Red actions: selected poems 1960–1993 / Robert Kelly.
        p.   cm.
    ISBN 0-87685-977-5 (paper : alk. paper). — ISBN 0-87685-978-3 (cloth trade : alk. paper). — ISBN 0-87685-979-1 (signed cloth : alk. paper)
    I. Title.
PS3521.E4322A6   1995
811'.54—dc20   95-35351
                                                                              CIP

To my wife
Charlotte
This work and its life

I have battled all day against colors
using only the sound of water, the roar
of seals, the rattling plumage
of funeral cormorants hung out to dry

and still every leaf mumbles green green green
and things once seen stay in the mind
burning like Troy but burning forever.

Table of Contents

RED ACTIONS

Selected Poems 1960–1993

Measure Those Distances

Of this night

        Here and now she becomes alive
     a roar of things out of the streets
     for the first time covered with skin
moving for the first time with the train of waters
     here this body is me
and this is why corners are bent and
this is the tunnel of her violent approaches
being out in the open without terror
being out in the parklands hunting for meat
being atlantis unresurrected and carelessly swimming
being navies and heavily-armed convoys
     being decked out with banners being
        sudden in an animal, being dark
being stone steps being broken on the
steps being thirsty and savage on the steps
being steps and an entrance to a living house
to be rain and twisting animal and a full skin
long hair hands trembling legs peaceful in bed
     her madwoman's hair and the air it floats on.

The church

stood deep in woods.
There were thorns
at its side and the ground
around it was broken,

very loamy, very brown.
No one to be there, say
mass there, rest there,
piss against a wall for

a hundred years. It was
the first church in these
mountains and wasps
lived in the eaves.

It was not a good place
to be at. The old paint
was still white; trucks
chugged along under the hill.

The boat

floated in the cove
her cat in it
keeping out the
shipped water

she sat up to her
ankles in slosh
and dreamed over at
Pennsylvania

where there are pines
and wildcats and
barns caved in on
empty mangers empty

troughs and she said
what is that star?
pointing to a single
light a farmhouse

way up the same hill
my father one year saw
a white enormous
silent owl nesting on.

Going

If you ever get there
where I have been once or
twice before, running in
summers with no sleep

under iron bridges, the
eddy around me, curve
of blackwillow bank
around me lying at bottom

looking up at the river's
skin, shadows of fish
in the sun and no whispers,
under wooden bridges

rumbling under the Fords
sifting dust into that

coolness of underbridge
striped with sunlight

God I love you all and
don't want you to be there
under the blue skin
itching in shallow grass

no thought in your minds
but to measure those
distances, counting
in pores of sunburnt skin

and tell me you're there
in inches and feet and
how very far away, easily
that much further away.

from ARMED DESCENT (1961)

Poem for the Jews

The candles of the Jews are ignited
tallow and paraffin stand tall in the darkness of Friday

In the sabbath lights are created and the Jews regard one another
and their eyes are like rockdoves moving from light to light

The fingers of the Jews dapple in fat from the lovefest
their fingers are white and immaculate stiff with the tendon of kashruth

The gentile walks among them
his heart filled with tolerance and his belly with spoiled meat
his eyes beg for the beginnings of love and dinners
beg for the cup of impossible seders for the endless givings of Jews
beg for the cleansing knife and merciless gestures of fingers

Jews wake up in the sabbath and their stomachs are empty
and there is not a sound of music and they polish their cars
and drive twelve sabbath journeys in sandals to the mountains

Jews rush along highways and see the fields but their eyes look ahead
towards the green lawns and tennis courts and white dresses
the ease of men walking the earth in the cool of the evening

In the sabbaths lights flicker on candles
Jews move quietly through mountains and across lakes

and over bridges and carefully through small streams
and their hands have given everything away and still keep moving
And if you love me take with both hands

At every second the Jews are created
at every second they are newborn and their eyes are filled with
          wings
and their hands have given everything away.

Sun of the Center

a man divided into animal
biting down through burrows with its teeth
into animal pressed into earth
a different shape
the five arrows of his motion
fly out into the structured world and are lost
the stone arrowheads enter the house of the wind
the reed shafts burn in the sky the lightning is random
proceeding from the north the black lightning out of a clear sky

into the shape of a man
who walks out with flowering skull and starfish fingers
and clay runs out of his nostrils
and his hips are still covered with bark
who makes patterns on the walls, his five fingers spread
who twists his hands together folding the fingers together
the true gesture of sunrise, the flower delivered from earth
who knows that empty horizons come from an open hand
who holds tight, who breathes on his own hands some cold
        morning
imperially able to make suns rise by being there and being himself
spread out in a blossoming cross against the black sky

into yellow flowers and the spell is lost things keep growing
a circular motion between earth and flower that must be plucked

that must be pulled out of earth and held in the hand
and what stays in the earth is brittle and breaks open
the dry stalk snaps
the dry pods of the tree split open
the dry beans inside them hard to the tooth
and the acorn pulled out of burnt grass after rainstorms
green cup crisscrossed crown split open by fingernail
the bitter interior kernel of roasted earth
bitter alum of earth puckering puckering and breaking open
the vegetable forests where he cannot live
the dying leaf the wooden stalk
hardening from within, brittle
which stand up out of earth and are wasted
brown at the edges the color of earth but the impulse
wasted, the somersault of the seed ended in mid-air
no ground to fall back to perishing in air

into the hot wind
that plays over the grains of soil
and lies down in hot sunlight and is called dog
and falls over itself in the mountains and is called river
and spreads out over the earth and is very close to being alive
but let only him whose body is of earth exist and sing
the shape of a man proceeds from all sides to center
and he is the star whose body is called movement
and in his hands the sun puts out branches
leaves and petals break out of silver
the corn is eaten, the animal howls, the sun flowers.

The Alchemist

the origin, far side of a lake
is always shadow

                    the voice goes around
                    it easily in one hour

given: man, the
origin, dark side of a lake, the sun
breaks on it, walks in it, drives
out the human face

the sun walks in the deep water
where the shadow of origin touches bottom

the lake silent in a cold without snow
where the further shore is invisible & there are
no hills   but cranes
spread out on it if there are cranes
if there is anything for them to eat
                    IF ANYTHING GROWS THERE

(making me whatever I do,
where he is or is about to be
not even letting the long afternoon grow under him)

SINCE OUR OWN EYES ARE NOT STILL
a song that some of us are singing in the ditch . . .
totum incognitum
sum of what we don't know for ourselves)
of ourselves

      the inquisitor's faces
      sheathed in rare earths,
      the old religion, our
      god in his own horns, a
      spring freshet in Spain
      uncovering Altamira,
      baring elements in

The alchemist
(twenty years over the alembic)
his left hand fisted, snotrag on cheekbone,
who shall weep
           and wake up in the morning
selling flowers in the veins of his arm
crying down the street jonquils jonquils
the needle stuck in his brain
inventing true north

      as the Chinese the southpointing carriage,
      the wheeled car with a figure that
      would go on forever pointing south,
      however the cart was turned

or Sung and Wei divided, north by south, Sung & northern
     Wei.

Sung: Mu Ch'i and his permissions, a measurement of light

     remote from Tao: contained

made into a thing

(six things, and a painting is not about them)

       but the task of a carriage is to go on riding north
       wherever the figure is pointing is south

& ride northward through the hemispheres of his brain
apple in the cracked skin . o madness

       will we reproach burnt flesh with a mirror,
       turn away Antichrist, reject the imposed form,
       with a clear clean painting however composed
       or organized, if the light be anything else but
       fragment?

& if we do not get up and destroy all the congressmen
turn them into naked men and let the sun shine on them
set them down in a desert & let them find their way out,
north, by whatever sexual power is left in them, if we do not
seize the president and take him out in daytime and show him
the fire & energy of one at least immediate star, white star,
hammer that down in his skull till he can hear only that
rhythm & goes and enters the dance or makes his own,
we will walk forever down the hallways into mirrors and
stagger and look to our left hand for support & the sun
will have set inside us & the world will be filled with Law,
and it is that exchange we must sweep out of the temple,
the changing of gold and power & the figure of Christ into Law,
till the leaf is subjected only to the patterns of its own green veins
which out of all patterns only will feed it when I am dark

light contained in the persimmons, six powers of light

folly of alchemists
stretched out on the snow
unlivable abstraction of his skin

in the robe covered with suns, moons,
motions we call "planets" and do not know
the green life in their valleys, geysirs
of wet light at the exact temperature of orgasm,
brown breath, brown blood wreathing the heart muscles

he holds to his eye

The alchemist

at the top of her A her
voice, breaking.

Calaf's name is "Love"

Stir well little
chew thoroughly
boy in the fire/
to sing in the
fire

where the streets run north
roughly but Broadway to the true north?
and asked
what corner is he on today with his music?
He was here yesterday and
sold daffodils

NAME IS LOVE

movements somewhere in time

since our own eyes are not still

in the sleepless dark
to travel with made light

holds his hand to his face & weeps for the lost struggle
wasted in the snowfall in the crucible, only the fire of Law
burning off sulfur & mercury and this fire is earth's face

      recognizable in the plain light
      the failure of self to go into gold,
      unaccountable. The alchemist

weeping in the Spanish field
in a cloak chewed into rags by its symbols

            a body,
            under it,
whose name is love & which only of all light love can eat

Hui-neng Chops Bamboo

To know it is to know everything
bamboo itself is used to make

especially that four-holed flute
with a note like wind under water

few Westerners can play

•

Of the strokes that can make up the picture
many, as if casually, combine
to shape the radical *chin*, "axe."

•

Such a small hatchet,
so few bamboo!
         How will we
ever fill up a picture with that?

•

He crouches in the grass. That
stupid grin. The razor in his
fist. He pounces on bamboo.

•

We have our own mountains.
I lived a summer on one and never
chopped wood.
                        There was a
lake and I chose to drink
hair-flavored water from my hat.

•

To walk one hour in those
mountains was enough

and filled my dreams with
dark trees. I could not grasp

the shape of a single tree or
what it had to do with darkness

or itself. Many trees and a black
sky. A tree is never alive.

Dreaming of branched lifeless things
with sap inside them I got up

from my particular sleep. Six o'
clock. I went out and turned my

flashlight on eight deer under
appletrees, obviously eating apples.

•

The chips fly! That
old man can really chop
bamboo!

•

Some trees have leaves
Some trees have butterflies

Hui-neng's bamboo is
marked "bamboo."

From any two, not one, iso-
lated passages the full
meaning of the picture is
conveyed. What's the rest for?

The radical "axe," the character "bamboo"

That is a picture of
Hui-neng chopping bamboo.

•

After you move the blade it
starts to move by itself.

It is like riding home
fast asleep and getting there

and knowing about it only when
the others get off and leave you alone.

•

It is not a puzzle it is
necessity

                as bamboo leaf
fits and is severed from bamboo.

from The Exchanges: Section V

                    a black flower
                            (charmed as night: we
            bring home apples & onions
                            your breath
            full of growth, roots
                    piercing into air, leaf
            yellow with a heart of rot,
            the shoot whole, still green
                    am I alive in your breath?
            green as the white juice of milkweed
            when you are talking
                            grows in my eye
                    I lie in night grass
                            can I tell you
            of all the plants of night, each
                    different from the daytime flower
                            dark orchids in the sickroom
            (the patient turning, soaked into the flannel)
                    poisoning the air?
                            or look out
            & see only the first black flower growing rounder
                    having at first 10 petals like a daytime flower
            & then a hundred petals, sharp, hard
                    knives of black grass beginning to turn
            & call it the only sun I see

there is no light
    you are in another room & I am dark
& am in the cup of a flower)
                where the milkweed
sturdy & spongy grows green in the lots
        (I cannot give up
    my childhood of vacant lots & empty houses
            the clock ticking in the empty room
    four o'clock)   out in the sun
Gerritsen avenue & a live horse groaning from the stable
    worn out already in the morning sun &
moving out towards us

                fields near the beach
    (when the stalk snaps, cells burst,
            spray in the air, the sweet juice
    chewed into my mouth
                am I doing this?
    these stalks of memory shatter
my mouth filled with glass)
        & one great black flower in them
                visible far out at sea
    on the barges a man sits
dabbling his feet in the cove & says
        "time to go in" & has seen the flower
        (the flower has eaten your father,
        cuts down your house & there are
strangers moving in the empty rooms
        the radio plays, the clock beats)
from which the horse himself has grown
            alive & broken, waiting
the flower of his mouth to open & swallow me
                for he is good
        & walks all day in the echo of its leaves

& begins to run & the driver falls into the wheel)
   power brakes . moving through suburbs
   red houses, another city, graveyard
   where they buried your father, crumbled into pieces,
      buried deep)
            near the beach where my
classmate Kent did drown & was grappled for,
hook entering the watery eye, &
      who was thereafter buried in a silken box,
      white, & mourned for,
            in whose rites
I did stand, all the boys of the class together,
an honor guard, & realized shortly that we
      did honor him not for his incredible sales
      of green desirable Victory stamps
            but for his death
in an afternoon after the season
            (the smell of that death
      was not worse
            than silence or a
                  bowl of fennel
      (sweetsmelling & green & yellow
         leaves bent over the table like a willow)
            brown & yellow on the fourth day)
                  into the water
            the same knife
      petals
         as circles move
                  (the long white
tunnel of the conduit out into the cove,
pumping sewage, &
            it was a road
to walk on like a leaf's edge
      out . away from the center

                    from grass & flowers & into
what does lie there when the night is still
& the dark room presses around me & I cannot breathe
& know within an inch of my face or my arm's reach
a great black flower spreads open like a mouth closing
          & the last thing I can hear is your breath

The Law

your body stands silent

I can feel the space of air
between the curved line of your back
& the rough brick you stand against

shaping that warm enclosure
the live proportion
the house of your time
against the wall,

you bring the room up to your hips,
it is space you talk of,
measurements your legs make
pivoting
your body sways
a true solid
never balanced,
force & battle & the sweetness of this hour,

figures the floor crosses
as you step
understanding, knowing the weight of things

& when you are movement the rain falls

An Epitaph

what to say of it
that long walk
in the street when
men are present,
walking alongside
with never a word
passed, no word
that passes as
coin, currency of
speech, believed

what to say of me
who walks "in the
company of flesh and
blood," knowing
not seasons & not
the tides

   a time for
wrapping the tree
close, time for pruning,
a time to look at
blossoms, the gathering,
to eat & the tree stands

full as before

I have eaten flowers
& I will die

Dr. Sunyata's Poem

asking that purple flower,
michaelmas daisy,
by whom it is sustained
& how,

     the answer flourishes.

it is known here
by some other name.

The Process

how much more
will I see
or see again:

the problem
hurts, I have
no eyes to

see it, no
flesh or time
to see it

through. A day
walks from sun
to shadow

on grass wet
from a last
sweet rain. It

solves itself
outside me
in the air.

I am with

from HER BODY AGAINST TIME (1963)

the old men
watching one

spring go out.

By the River

at just such hour
the mist walks
shattered on the field

the world & the wind
move,
it is an hour birds
turn overheard

wings fold unfold
a swallow tail
notched clear, sky
inside it,

they fly in threes

six birds four by
two, four breaks,
two trinities glide by

upriver away from
where I watch each
three join that

from HER BODY AGAINST TIME (1963)

great wavering
horizon of birds,
gone, trees
hold the long field

& looking back
over my shoulder
even I can see

a whirlpool of early
evening gnats
silently involving air,

dark soon
& no order

To Her Body, Against Time

Long over, what's on the tree
shivers. Sky hides behind
white-faced, giving flesh to branch,
a red leaf

or yellow far enough away,
what Broch called "the style
of old age," simplified
of images,

lean in the perfection of the bough,
naked & half-undone. Clouds break,
rain against a hidden sun,
the form plain

from HER BODY AGAINST TIME (1963)

Haruspex

Examine the skypath of sightless birds
drawn by the currents of
                    historical
                    acts, air, responding to the limits of
any living body, channels of energy.

Birds, sink down for the food spread here
that auguries be taken from what you pluck & what neglect,
          cold stone, the seed hulls
                    shaken down, blown to the ground,
this empty wind.

                    I found I had written:
                    "Later I watched a river
                    that rippled as your flesh did
                              or does, the skin of it"

& pecked around for a house for it,
          prepositional,
                    putting one thing before another,
                    unmerited.

                              The metaphor
walks there, blue tail stiff out behind him, scratching at
          what I put there, not before,

        chasing him away so I could offer,
alienate those seeds
                    & what flows in them.
The birds are in one tree now, neglect, neglect, how many
hours blind here in darkness,
        afraid to turn the light on,
                not every augury, not any
prophecy worth enduring,

                        but in the sun the bluetail comet walks
& lights the unmerited night with, augury, our common blood,
        what flows
                in us as in them,
                        that river I could not
        see without seeing,

                    who?
                        birds,
        spell out the answer to.

Reaching the Limits

Out of the city, non-human reek elaborate
in the shunned air. Driving out in brick heat
       the scattered trees explaining
       the structures of Pindar
turned outward from the common measure, a tower
but a tower only of light. We see.
If the soul does not see, no wind blows rain fall
& the steps go up, into the sunlight, banished in the bright eye.

We see the mortal brightness of the sun crackling
through the young willows. We see. Perishing eyes,
perishing lungs, perishing hands. I thought I told you not to
       touch me.
Be grateful I have hands. Or touch me. Do you know
how it is to be touched this way, killed by a bird cry
coming too soon? The soul, seeing into you. Make them stop.

All day the soul sings for a breath of air, prances to breezes,
vomit its quick learning in the caressing shade.
       the problems
       of Pindar's melody
       or to grasp
      a complex order
outside the easy music of the head. Or let it touch me.

Face in the Rock Wall

                                        sun about to rise
                                        be kind to
                                        all those who cannot

face in the rock wall
face in the rock all
rock has faces

                    it is heavier
                    to refuse
                    to see them

than not to hear
music,

        as from a preliminary age undocumented by direct data
        the troop of Atlantean musicians comes,
        brass kettledrums, copper lyres, flutes calling
        in what sounds like language, the bray of meaning.

        or are they musical brazen liars out of Besant's thought
        Blavatsky put there, a realization, if tawdry,
        of the meaning of that splendid hidden dark im-
        ponderable Plato
                        we see in his Dialogues like a rough

but recognizable face in a rock wall,
                              all rocks in their
weatherings take on faces
                    that change as the sun moves
or we walk past
              to be no face at all)

                                        that hard face

in Franconia
I dreamed inside me
knowing,
knowing through me
its way to the world
              grinding its wheat)
                                    the weight
of their music
              on us
                    (my dream
                    under the ground
                    a city
                    right on top of me
                                      southward the lake
in whose only waters I could breathe.

[a gathering of lunes from the first years]

they are given to
hold close, not
air, not each other

•

thin sliver of the
crescent moon
high up the real world

•

in that air between
your knees the
song begins to sing

•

after silence your legs
break open
the final measure

•

close black eyes intent
on danger
me, of all people

•

birds come down to feed
no other
business on this earth

•

Is this form too long?
Belshazzar
left before the end

•

Out of the sea comes
Venus to
quench one final thirst

•

Is this form too short
Love alone
could make do with less

•

you taste of fish that
swim where no
boat ever passes

•

this night conceals no
animal
body but my own

from Up on Autumn

...
red cow
a longhorned
sun,
            hairy
it's hairy

phantom-fighter
she gives milk

dispelling
reality in reality
one for another
turned or turned aside,
the
        real is
        where you find it
la la la
in which specific lyre
tunes
three strings
or seven,
                box turtle
                sound box
amplifies the

note does not enlarge
the air
          as built
on such impoverished means
stays upright
          veering neither to right nor to left
the castle
of the specific man
plucks that instrument's
particularities

                    All
                    Cows
                    Eat
                    Grass

taught to intone
spaces on the infernal staff
commodious of mistake

the locus
of these times
at the Limit of Contraction
Adam
          beyond which
whom
          none could fall
& will write as difficult
songs as I want
meant song
song bravely la la,

in the spaces of music
taught to sing
or cantor tuneful
one octave down

                    Spi
                    no
                    za
yoohoo
you who
toutes vaches mangent l'herbe
                    (Tempestuous
                    Volatile
                    Mercuri-
                    hermetic
Mercurius seipse Hermes
in
              time vines meet happily
time vaunts moldy hours
& God is present in
every hand,

                                        will eat
this winter mild herbs
and chew
this night
substantial bread
quiet beer
at kitchen
table, dark out-
side but light in here,
who rose up early
months before
to harvest
when Pleiades rose
above his
eastern trees,
              & the cow
              heroine of this

        piece before
will last the winter

. . .

lyre
locus
horned cow
from the skull of a lyre-horned cow
a lyre be made:
mastic to plug the nose & mouth
a wooden peg beneath the cerebellum
& from the eyes
the music flows

what do I know of Jews in fall?

safe in the barn
the cow chews
all winter long

the skull is the place where time walks
all in the evening
up & down
Spinoza's head on Adam Qadmon's head is
placed
& time shows through them clearly colored
I turn the pages to come to the first head
I turn to an empty page

my mother did not hear
about her father's death
until the milk was
flowing well

& I was growing blindly

          the skull is the lyre on which time plays
          & is its proper instrument
the spaces
in the staff
its care

to specify
redeems,
to seed the
ground
with facts
burns
impurity
from the
soil,
        catch
the single
at the door
of the exact

o Adam would have made a slender gypsy
commodious of resentment
too slow to steal
he sat & named the animal he couldnt catch

       built
on such im-
poverished
means,
chastel
orgeluse

pride's house
above & below
a fact
a tree
east
of the lawn
west of the
stars

time veers me home
the triple bronze
hammered
to look like cow
up on autumn
pastures
brown
this one death is the death of all . . .

State of the Nation

summer is walking out & Master Horse
rides with sun on his back
down across the wind bound yellow grass
brown green burnt grass at summer's
margin
      I read a parable beside his text
the thrown-alongside, the message
coming at me edgewise, on, Great
Summer is dead in the forest, Great
Yellowface Summer with green silk robe
rots in the mud beside the thin brooks
& all his green blood turns to red
              He is
Father, we greet his body stretched
like a shadow over our imagination
dying capaciously with much noise
his message half out of his pocket, leaves
rustling like unread pages of a will
jibber around his dead hair
           Great Summer
is dead & his uncle the crazy horse
rides screaming over the corpse
The nine mens Morris is fild vp with mud
this last year he lived

quietly with occasional prance
& never led the dancers to green places,
his silence has unhinged the season

Master Horse's great iron mouth
chews the ball of the sun
long shadows distorted from their source
run over the plain grass
                              out of the woods come
all the sons to dance around their father

We have no ritual of the reborn sun
we came here in darkness two months over
wild seas with never a taste of sun,
                              by that
neglect & all that we deprived
to make ourselves a nation we have lost
all need for sun

                    we say *sol-stice*
when sun stands, & have no sense if up
or down or back or forth or living or
dead, it is a term in the imagination,
nobody sees it, nobody sees the
sun rise in his own heart, in his
own eyes after

Weep summer dead among the sunflowers
yellow leaves stippled with green, Summer
dead in a new car up Mt Rutsen road
where lovers come to work their business
that is love, love with windows closed
& Summer dead slumped over the wheel,

horsehead autumn running under the full trees
one after another, dodging from sun to
shade to sun, turning, & they cant evade
the coldness of his life

                    which lives
inside them too, & all of us who wear
sunglasses in the sun
                    I stopped the car
before the upgrade to fit my sunglasses on
awkward, dropping the lenses, to fit new
lenses on my eyes, I do not want
the sun in my eyes,
                    this setting sun

America was founded in drizzle
a sprinkle of rain
everything drizzles down to us
cool & sequestered from fire,
                    the witches
praised their god & his powers: his
nature was colder than any man's, that
intercourse sustained them, they loved that
passion only when the prick was cold
the ice right up to their hearts
                    They
were our progenitors, they & their
daughters & their quiet husbands useful
around the house & compliant in bed, made
white church'd america, made the isolate
steeples leaping hollow cold & heavy
lead-roofed into leaden new england sky,
a picture I saw as a child, called Xmas.

Whose mass is christ's mass when our
lord the sun hangs in the sky all morning
lifeless in the well of sky
                    Will I pretend
to worship the unconquered sun when inside me
is cold disdain, immaculate seclusion
a bright solid like the masculine moon?
I am a child of those christmases, the snow
on the ground my joy & the tracks in the
snow that lead me to the darkest part of the woods

      Master Horse
      sprouts his horns
      & leads his poets
      into dance

      they sing the
      song he laid
      on them, his
      blessing they
      call it to dance

      they dance
      their flesh trembles
      in their pants
      under a solid moon

We are its parents and originalls

Summer is dead & the american intellect
grows quiet & white in the shadow of big trees,
cold & delicate our whimsy, our senses
turned to the inside of the vein
                    James &

Howells & Clemens & Jewett
tune their fiddles to a diminished air,
to the tinking of moorish bells, the leaping
dancers of the morisco,
crash of the flamenco snares
Prescott refuses to enter Spain
lest the sight of those places rob him of
his flawless knowledge of what happened there,
Thucydides whittles
in the corner by the stove
Trilling & Barzun play
checkers with hooded eyes
it is somewhere in Connecticut
it is the shadow of another time,
the hi-fi prances *Dixie*,
                    Henry Thoreau
                    walks in the woods,
we poor white trash linger
in the shadow of big buildings
unsettled by a fitful wind,
                    over Japan
                    two symbols
of our condition never blow away,
there is no empty air

                    Now the elves
have borne father Summer's body off,
come is slimy on the plastic seats,
the radio dreams on
                    The rickety shack
where our mind is at home shudders
under the hoofbeats of that crazy animal
carrying the darkened sun
                    his masked rider

down out of sight in the fertile ground
In the white church they are singing
a german hymn, Alleluia Alleluia
to no purpose, the priest in his pulpit
looks back at the people, their feet
are perfectly still.

XVIII: The Wood Man

Lightly he comes to the end of the book
filled with the technical harmonies, *dákrüa*,
these are the waters he weeps,
his eyes express,

at first, the young ones, *dümp'nai*,
only the young ones, Tender & sweetsmelling,
cotton & linen, veils of a single
movement in all of them, bodies,

Lightly the woodman came to his own house door
& went outside, out of the wood of his days
to the place where the people bathed
ordinary under waterfall, a mist of spray
prickling the dusty leaves, *poikilot'rón*, hillocks
they sat on, took human shape, took
the mind's eye of the woodman, his eyes,
his mind.
　　　　Harmonies, classical, harmonies
he will not hear again. Now the madman
is a man without ground-note, no constancy
sings itself in its head. He hears everything, sees
all the goatfoot leaves and bushes dancing, sees bodies
everywhere & all time, hears all sounds & so
passes beyond harmony. The man is wood,

wood is mad, the woodman opens his heart
to the footsteps of all of them, they come through him,
they leave their traces, the leaves their traces,
doxa, all that the woodman, wood man
knows is mad stuff about the people's thighs,
wild surmises of their private parts, footsteps,
impressions in wet grass, spoor of his heart
(sad instrument) towards them, unrestrained, un-
founded in the fact of their flesh, his opinions.
                                                    Skin
of them through the leaves, some brown, some white.
But wood is matter, his material, bones of his house,
he follows the lines in the ancient book, comes to the end
& comes again. Being outside his house, out
in the damp air, *psük'e*, which is his breath breathing,
shaping a pass of his eyes from torso to torso,
all of them dancing before him in the wood, not one
close enough to touch.
                              He finds the words around him,
where can he hide, *k'oría kai ta dendra*
ouden m'et'elei didáskein, hoi d'en tô astei
ánt'ropoi, nowhere to hide, where will he cherish
the pages of his book, nowhere to cherish them,
no place of moss, no shelter of dry leaves. Their voices
pull at his wood mind, "Find it in us," they say,
"find it all in us, find us all where."
Tears of the woodman, the motions of his soul
compelled his eyes, he heard the words, closed
his book and looked out at the company of footsteps.
"We are the harmonies," they sang, their place
was a green glade laid out to dance on, *k'óros*,
an empty place.
                        Whatever he chooses, will the wood,
the wild wood, still unlopped branches, all

that uncut timber let him build, give him bones
for his house and more than his house? Flowers at the door
of his cabin, portulaca, borage, impatiens
russet gorgeted under his shade.
                                        Dancers run away. "Find us,
find us and know us if you can." He builds a house
on their dance floor, paces it out in true measure,
holds the words in his mind and the wood in his hands,
dákrüa, subdues his tears. "They will dance here,"
he says, breathing hard as he can. Their limbs in the leaves.
His mind sees the harmonies, *tek'né*, the grain of the wood
& the work's own way, wet way. Beyond the door,
the madman watches them dance in the wood's grain.

•

> *Fields and trees have nothing to teach me—my teachers are*
> *in the city, people.*
>   Socrates in the Phaedrus

[from the Book of the Kings, the Five-line stanzas]

saw light
in shape
of bird,
sparrow
from winterdark

through light
of man hall
out, enough
to change his
manners,

bloodless offer,
drink this light
mindful of me
diathekê,
his blood

like Aga
Memnon's
eventually
is sea,
sea

your portion,

king of men.
...
we leave him
long time
considering
a silken
rug

(crimson
bordered our dream,
the moon
overthwart
the sea)

from back
to his right
a presence:
another door,
entered & was

Agamemnon
in his bath,
soap-cuckolded
slain
by a nameless

demon
of woman's unease,
hungering
for oracles
he laid

hands on sibyl
to possess

the end
of all prophecies,
the journey home.
. . .
passions
betray us,
destroy us,
rock
is enough

ylang ylang
verveine
santal
rigorous
absence of free

alkalis.
Salitter,
the salty
quality
of God,

freedom
now.
"See him?"
she said,
"he's dying,

dirty old
man all the
hoarfrosts"
winters
of the world

poured
through his mouth,
this king
of frozen time,
and the green

eyed one
rose from her couch
& murdered
oriental
Agamemnon,

his black hair
like a rose
wilting
in the scummy water
of his bath

. . .

But to the beloved
"child of Hermes
and Osiris"
the sparrow
hastening from winter

brought the news
of light:
"the people
inhabit the streets,
eating

flesh & not flesh,
tamarind juice

& heavy
with poppies
forge

passports of his dead
state,
barricades broken,
oranges
rot at their feet

the people
eat"
All this he saw
in the rug,
turned

back from the door.
Drugs
do not work:
we know that
& we persist,

aspirin &
ethanol,
leaves
of the trees
if

we are anything
we are flowers,
annuals,
blooming &
withering

but root
persists
stem rises
again & again
always

an identity
outward
from spring
a while
fall,

fragrance
of whose acts
particular
to be
consumed.

A Lesser Art

call
& wait for an answer

let the words
come

inside you
settle
where they
choose

or let them go
dance
as their mode is
or mood

do not pick
to make
what you think
you know

they will say
you better
than you know

and as for critics
shun
even this

(or conceive a Persian poet
heavy with wine & contentment

who turned to his lover, his
body idly stirring up musk as he turned:

I would have gone outside to smell the first roses
But doors are compromises

A Spell

Someone immensely naked:
it is that, tree,
I summon from your shade

opening the gates . love,
a confluence of people

on the one silver road,
pathways of order,
                    the company!

must make, must be
beyond what we are trained to take

as beauty,
beauty being the quality

or immensity of our undress
& we can talk to each other

when what we are doing is the milky way
travelling hand to mouth forever with our beautiful eyes.

ॐ

Against death this density
overlay of grasses,
lords, the richness of your fields

men and woman walking in them
not
the evening, not even the harvest

but in the middle of our time

world we know something of & go
to sleep taste of on our tongues

from Alpha

I.

kept coming back because of the softness of our skin
knew what would become of us

& now while the night flamed down in Boston
it was morning on the other side of New York
& the softness of our skin knew what it had come for

the risk was terrible & all our joy

this was the classical story (pigeons
& child murderers in the park)

& meant that literacy gives an awful power
o cavatina of our sickness o stretched out lyric of our

shared pathologies
our! (Rockies & false syntax)

ocean!
indecent pacific!

my body naked under leather
crushed in the machine it had always become

2.

back in the days I knew us the sea was wet
the sea made certain

specific philosophies of roses
flourish at the edge of itself

metropolis of waves
unsymmetrical wave of our most rigid sleep

& we were wary of the undertow
ride with it we said

fall into its own security
rhythm rhythm we kept remembering

it was our passion to do things at the surface of our skin
& would not have thought to mention it again

except pornography is the cure for war

3.

it is a branch in february
& it commits adultery

even a little while after the sun rises
our acts with one another are sheathed in ice

namelessly shining

baffled by adverbs
our orgasms wait for us at the end of the world

4.

our speech says the breast
of the newfallen snow

an old story talks about three
drops of blood upon it

like the cheeks of an almost remembered lover
feverish in the diseased

dismembered memory

as if our abstract earth
put on flesh sometimes

or as it really is
that I came here from some other City

stood naked among travelers at the terminal
and my only speech was blood.

Prefix: Finding the measure

Finding the measure is finding the mantram,
is finding the moon, as index of measure,
is finding the moon's source;

                    if that source
is Sun, finding the measure is finding
the natural articulation of ideas.

                    The organism
of the macrocosm, the organism of language,
the organism of *I* combine in ceaseless naturing
to propagate a fourth,
                    the poem,
                              from their trinity.

Style is death. Finding the measure is finding
a freedom from that death, a way out, a movement
forward.

          Finding the measure is finding the
specific music of the hour,
                    the synchronous
consequence of the motion of the whole world.

Stanzas from Dante

Verge in me, matter, I feel you tell me, feel
whom he lay, and after, who came as Creature
determinate, fixed, detained by counsel,

to see who lay there, all human nature
noble as the sea, keel to his fated
noonday's oarways, how parted from her fades.

Null winters do sear such and more,
pearl low sky cold under the terms of space—
Go see it germinate, or quest a flower

which stays always new, meridian fact, say
this charity oozes into mortal eye
seeing die spirits and fountain vivacity.

Thunder, say the answer: one day a gentle valley
will equal vault-grazing Everest—one recurrent
truth is an answer: all Will would our senses deny.

The Death of Rasputin

He couldnt open the wine, drank
the brandy. A list of bad
angels from the book of Enoch.
Waters of the sea. Neva. *We live*
on the inside of some world.
It is not a star.

Shot seven times in the spine
he staggers through the courtyard
looking for a fire or a map
of Egypt or hem of the Virgin's
robe or a new blue suit. Knives
reach up to cut him, cyanide
kills the rats in his body.
Clubbed down to his knees at last
he remembers a song
                              Holy mother
meek & mild
                    come protect your
dying child.
                    The angels wait
for him where the river thaws,
months away. They are patient.
They all have corkscrews,
napkins, each wine inside its

appropriate glass. Room left
on the menu they include
remorse. Or the death of Rasputin.

Across the frozen river naked
girls walk backwards. Any minute
they will be here. Or there.
The bells ring. The confused
testimony of his assassins
fills his ears. *Why am I dying?*

Someone chops a hole in the ice
& dumps him in. He says
something about love, then dies.
No one hears it. He does not
understand it himself.

Alba

the sun
didnt know a
thing

all of a
sudden
Krakatoa

of the cock's
crow
& the light

lit
my lady a-
waker than I

lush at my
side
said "I

am spring
green
after all

day misty

rain"
she kissed

her finger
tips
lingered

on our lips
the sun
not yet

able
to do a thing
to us

but show us
ourselves
of all things

after so
much knowing
most

clear
& most dear
to partisans

of infinite
touch
such

harvest to our
lust this
new mown sun.

Last Light

there is a meadow
where the grass is now

& then every time,

that older than Christian
moment
            when Christ hangs on his cross
& the world is still

no one knows
if he grieves or rejoices
hangs conscious or asleep or already
dead,

bugs dance,
sun a while set
but sky over west
almost hurts to see
blue going to apple green going to red,

stratus salmon red
in the last light

if I fix wide open eyes

on the mountains' sharp crest
I can make light
rise again from the west,
but just for me

the bugs of night
unfamiliar shapes, dont bite yet

I have believed in time
& in time
come

to this meadow
where all the
moments of time are one

Lao-tze saw these pines
Adam this river,
an 18th century Adam
decorous & white
saw it flowing
his waters away
out
into ocean,

saw
his garden as no more
than source of the stream

watches
it pass

to America the tide
a girl & boy

come from the woods

pines now black
I can look at the sky

on the lawn
one dandelion
puffball stands immensely alone

like feather-horned Venus
rising behind me
empty sky still light
but not as light as she

almost all
the light lives in the river

in front
of the agony of any being
we are stupid mute,

what is important to each man
he never says,
never learns it till the light
walks out of the sky
& he is left
alone with his failed utterance
impossibly clear in the dark

write everything
the oracle said,
Christ on rood road
tree over river
lovers behind the sundial by the pool,

everything I see or make or am,
seed spores of dandelion
holding light

let what is natural
say what it can

what is not here
is nowhere

men
should live in cities
shun
these ghostly edens of twilight
where all we have never been
mocks what we are

noble & foolish & dull
putting off our time of saying

when it is the uttering
not the knowing
that makes it so,

red is dying
pacific turncoat blue turns black

anyone watching me
would know nothing,
would see a dead man
whose hand moves on the paper,
he or the wind
occasionally turning a page

a moth
rises against cloud,
everything louder
under the trees

star out
straight up

above a dandelion
I can barely see

the splendid company of men who move in darkness
along a green continuity has nothing to do with time

for all we see we know nothing,
our utterance alone makes

something of this death,

Adam after hundreds of years
laying him wantonly down to rest.

Sonnet 18

for Nerval, le pendu

When they look they'll find it beautiful
if they find it at all, a hand
not getting any older, holding a weight
as a woman would hold a sword
tipping her hand to the power in it
                              The Cut.
Weight that a man could balance on a leaf
& still believe:
              that much music was left in him.
He started when he could. All the mythology
weighed him also down.
                        Fell & the grass was cool,
felt wet after the stone sky, intimate & free.
Which is all he could ever have wanted to become,
month after month all the way into evening,
stayed there forever & lifted the weight of the hand
he'd found beneath him, a skin he always knew.

Song XXI

Not ready lord not ready . I can't get started . blew sweet . out .
futter has a sound like an animal doing it . a church
of the brothers & the sisters,

                       also amen . at Roxbury
where on the hill

                    (clear view of the Naval Hospital) "best
place to defend the City,
                 Battlements & from"
                           presently known as
Roxbury Standpipe . to some
                       . to others less specific, the
ladies (bless em = apotropaic formula)
                      it was the 18th Trump
that conduit to suck down starfire & bed in
                    earth, menstruum
fire & aër, i.e.,
          a green-eyed tower, mother moon
above it
          (fancy! I was on the point of likening
the pale moon to her eyebrow, tower's,
                 phallos is woman & seeks
her own . (shining!) . witness: Ashera whore-devil of hill folk
whose prop was prick & whose device
                one upright unstripped sapling

from SONGS I–XXX (1968)

(old tree would do),

witness cycladic Afrodita, under form of an
unhewn stone, up-pronging, jagged,

or Hermes' oldest hallows:
column or quern, *herm*, that is

Hermaphrodite means
Hermes is Venus .

This . was the hill to cherish, earthworks here
subdue the city, ravelin straggling down the slope,

today
a dog jogs there seeking a master .

Black people move out of houses
& comprise the hill . I mean go up the hill,

wander
the circuit of the tower's base, old iron door bolted shut,
spikes driven in the masonry to hold it closed,

dry wood &
cold air in .

this is the point of likening, this is the world
inside the mirror that is the mirror, the world that is the world
but the way . of moving there . where . the light
chooses to begin

. it was sighting . along the finger
where at the edge of the desert

(Red Earth) scorched by Set's hand
the green began

& coming to the White Earth, the dead land, then
across the sea . is not a sea .

but the way . of moving
is . gold wire . the code spun on spirals of . gold wire
with Saturn's song . mark of Cain (Kane's mark, the eyebrows
of my mother's tribe, one down one up . dissolve but also
fix . settle here to flee . everywhere, wander,
shunted along the genetic warp . fix . cut loose . an identity

through time . across a sea . the sea is no sea
                                        . my eyebrow upward
from the terrestrial face .
                        I thought the preacher said Kane
I thought he meant my people were killers, murder people,
                                                me marked,
set to wander . but no man dare touch me . or I touch woman)
he did not lie,
                we kill & go on killing, the fingerprints
come true)
            the Nile is smooth & sluggish by Cambridgeport, thick
uncolor under Boston,
                    Set's hot breath across it, blasting Somerville
drying the wits out of Everett .
                                he spoke: How dare you not
live in cities,
                he spoke & all the gap-faced men of Lexington
shrank under the earthworks . bright sky over Medford .
                                                but the Nile
is torpid under River Street bridge . two poplars bend from the city
a girl beneath them, skirt alive in wind .
                                        I saw from the tower
"best place to arm the city
                        command all lowland" . embattled earth,
this . is an intercourse . fleshbreak . against the wall of the world
I cant get . started .
                    I read in a book how Horus futtered Set,
set his fish to swim in that dark water
                                (gust over the Charles,
sicksweet excitation of winter's end, that one soft wind
that blows then across the Sea of Reeds & never
                                        elsewhen) then the sun
rose, I saw my face
                set in the glass die in the glass but my eyes died last

94   *from* SONGS I–XXX (1968)

moon-capped tower clear . she dances . with the genetic code
unravelling in her hands . this
                              is the circle of the world,
circulus mundi . the endless cord loops upon itself . figure of *ankh*
but the loop grows smaller, the world
                                        castellate battlement
we see through to shoot . the city invested, Hermes is Venus,
I prop this stone up to
                          "save the city from the English
not ready lord not ready . lady . these eyes my towers . the world
folds in upon itself, circle
                              "best place to
no one could move in the city or come up the Harbor & we not
blow them out of the water out of the fire out of the air out of the
earth,
        Lord Aithêr do you hear me,
                                        we are not animals doing it,
the cloth of our will runs ragged, where is our national thought,
it was to come to a point .
                              genital organization, or by gender,
or by . the generations .
                            it was to come to a tower . above the whole
world . where the enemy troops my brothers were on the move
against my brethren . who were all I had .
                                            my sisters
who were as a well of sweet water,
                                      all this while I
thought the sun a lance . it is the gold
                                          heart of the target)
my brothers & sisters . who have I but yourselves
locked with me . within the circle of .
                                          & all of us killers, "the
city defended from this prospect .
                                    black Egypt . black Egypt .

sisters who have one   between you
                                    mouth . mouth .
(this is classicism, rift in the aithêr,
                                    ether riff
blow old white song)
                    in your mouth, one part between you all, among
. but what have I
                    but your faces, ancestors
                                    honoring
your minutest instructions I have
constructed this fortress overlooking the whole city & from the
earthworks can survey the movement of friend or enemy on the harbor
or sloop or merchant barge up river to the first cataract or
down seaside where it is said great Ocean is that rings us round

Injune

In June was a jar had
honey in its head.

I tell you the history of one
conspicuous jar, one long
derangement
like a song through a door,
a door ajar.

Door had
hardly opened
when

the honey in the jar would be a
history of our tribe, until
a young man got the honey
in his head.

June was this jar
how life began.

Breakfast was clotted milk
because the stars.

The bread was baking in the earth.

The hearth was never far.

Fire was never hard.
We cared our way in,
cool look of a June morning
I remember in July.

Milk & honey.
The jar was heaven
broke & poured down,
A man's life is spilled milk.

A boy saving rain

•

The stars were jars, were doors
& we kept looking back,
angel at the fiery gate,
boy, delivery boy, looking
down at his body,
down at the smashed quart.

This angel is this boy.
The doors are open all night long,
that's where the cool wind comes
that blows the honey into our heads,
is sleep.
Crust of vision on new-wakened eyes,
sleep in my eyes.

The head's on straight, the Lion
we see in the stars
reminds us of our own,

the girl was wise but inexperienced,
slipped,
they both got honey in the head.

But hers was heavier
& remembered earth
& all the caves
filled up with jewels, & gold
ran down into the ground to hide,
to be the secret content of her
honey thought,
her heavy head,
thinking grapes onto the vine
(wild
taste of the bitten apple)

his lion slipped, his lighter head
sticky with honey
stuck to the sky.
It was June. We were born.

The gold
hides in the ground

the way tomorrow's weather
hides in the air,

the way what I will finally know
hides in me now.

•

Injune is a verb, the way a word
makes flesh, is begotten not made.

Injune is our coming to this place.

On the Mayflower
we came to June.

The gates of Cancer
aim us at the Moon.

We act as if we came here to injune.

(Injune yourself!

It's wetter than you think.
The Queens of Oil
are melancholy,
the Kings of Honey
run to capture them,
shoot into their hives
a curious message
shaped like themselves.
Their joys arrive
& set fire to the sea.

•

Honey lasts forever,
Men can eat honey,
        Pelagius said,
& know themselves slowly,
meeting each act or fail-to-act
as the bee meets the flower,
capable by her nature
to choose the right one.

Sin would be not doing this.

The magical bees of the Island of Britain
sang in his head

where all the honey went
the sea-god his father sent

to nourish the chance
of human possibility.

All we can do is know what we do
& let the bees decide.
Tastes like honey.
                        In June the bees
are busy at the linden
I speak of an actual tree
rarer than remorse.

•

(On Narrative)

An angel came to me today & told me that my proud dislike of
narrative reveals an unwillingness to be accountable for my own
actions. I contended that narrative is mostly just greediness for
guilt. Storytellers fussily choose details. Let the selection be
natural (I punned), let what happens happen. Let what happens
reveal itself fully & truly in what happens next. If that were true
(he smiled) I would need only one pair of wings. You are in the
grip of a simplistic belief about causality, hence excuse yourself
from natural act. You think this causes that; not so—these
cause this. All these cause all those. The corn ripens in its
season and whether you want to or not, *you go with it* as it grows.

Look, I said, I hate the theater, I want *now* to turn into *then* in such a subtle way it feels like now all the time. I am only responsible for now. Now is my mother and my father. That's why I keep quoting Pelagius. Let the moment ripen—the grain is the same as the seed, the yield the same as the source.

The angel smiled again at me (as one smiles at a deft prevarication). That sounds nice, he said, but these three pairs of wings I am are to hide & reveal, to propel my intelligence through the enigma of time. Maybe to deny it at last, since the Work or Arcanum of angels is the End of Time. You are striving to assert that humans can wield an angelic intelligence, total in each motion. You think you can possess time, and make this now so wide it touches every then. Every one. You are just greed, I think, just another lover of time. You stall, you linger to slurp up the honey, you go to war and make philosophy and create gods and theologies just to keep the sun motionless on the mountain. You trust causality because you people are begotten, not created. We angels are created, and all our science is *will*. But not even we can will all ways at once, or even one way forever. Will-less, you drift and think you can choose the causes. Will-full, we move through the world and all we know is where we can go—our very movements are permissions. We can only move where all the rest is moving. Will-less, you move through a dream of forgiveness, and dare to talk to me about Pelagius! First of the self-styled Christians he was to make it plain that we are accountable for each act and each failure to act—*& are responsible for nothing apart from that.*

There's a war going on (I burst out), there's violence & stupidity, the planets run & recur in their dumb cycles, every jolt they give us spills over into war & cruelty. The sons of God who honor god in flesh & openness are everywhere slain & imprisoned. And not just now—it is at every stage of human history. How can we even have a right to walk on our feet on this continent where Cortez did what he did, where murder is the natural answer to every question, where the books of the Mayans were burned and black men were sold and young men are still made slaves of war? It was never different. In Pelagius's time citizens were enslaved, slaves bartered, rulers flayed alive. His God dies on the cross. What is the sense of narrative? What can it tell us the cemetery and killing fields forgot to say? We do not love, we do not live in honor. If there are causes, we have never deciphered them. If there is a cure, it has been hidden from the beginning of time. Why do men take pleasure in killing & destroying? What *is* that pleasure? Is history the name of it? Did anything else ever happen? The animal delights in its *here-&-now*, and we kill it. Our cortical memories which are supposed to be stocked with situational devices to protect us from contingency, are they anything really but treasuries of barbarous images, records of torture & dismay? If that is the world's will, I turn against it. I turn against history, against story, against time—I "turn my body from the sun" in search of the exact moment—even sunlight cannot find it there.

The angel seemed to pause now; at first I thought he was stuck for an answer. Then I knew he was waiting for my anger to simmer down—anger does no good. And this time he did not smile. These facts & stories in your mind, he said, are accurate enough. But where in any of them do you see anything but what a human did to another human? The tale of human horror has only one meaning—men did these things. And only one hope—men could *choose* not to do them. One at a time. No other way. But each could choose. What humans call Will is a joke, an unreal thing, a recorded tune a life keeps playing in the background while it jerks and trembles to the trembling of the net that is its life. Human will is what humans have always done. It is not a motive, it is an abstraction-from—a vector mathematicians could *infer* from human behavior. But that behavior can be changed. Consciousness has something to do. Is something to do. It takes a million years, maybe, but it took many millions for you to become the killers you are.

Or you are a jar into which all the honey of time has been poured. When time ends, the jar will break, & there will be left only the honey you've gathered or restored.

Of William Mount, the "Luminist"

There are dyes & there are textures:
these orbital continuities

these veins that we call planets
move in the permission of their single

Qualities, plexuses of a neurology
whose central brain is everywhere,

nowhere.

> That's what they were talking about,
> those strange people in the Essex woods
> (was it Apple street, or dirt-road off
> from the corner of Apple,
> anyway, nobis quoque they came,
> from Boston, peccatoribus)

> whose leader played the piano & hated the Moon

(that Moon
in Quidor's woods
were the same forest,
fox fire? or salu-
tation of the celestial

rot

 —lightbearer—

    outside the frame of the picture. The Americans
painted light
coming from outside the picture

      (Jefferson kept the first faith
that orient light would bathe this people)

        lodge light, the celestial
light trapped in the mason's stone,

      ashlar from Lucifer's crown
who was likewise a lightbearer,

     likewise morning & evening.

        'The Masses,
The Masses.'

    There was that hope or confident expectation
light from outside
the system into the system,

    as Mount's Setauket
a vase or vessel of such radiance
where only the woman is dark & spears eels in the lagoon
whereas the land no less than the water

      engorged with light
with which also the boy
—the generations!—

    is silently fulfilled.

The Moon

by early morning
is down the western
sky. It is white and
blue covers it

in cloud. Wherever
you look there is
something setting, some
tired back outstretched

resting from work you
never dreamed of. It
is further away
than any other time.

You reach out and
get nothing. Who are
you to judge these men.
They live here too

afraid to turn the
light off, just trying
to draw one late blue
breath. You still have

nothing, the moon has
set, the sun rises, leave
them alone, there is
nowhere else.

Mudra

The old book talks about the form,
double-pointed ellipse, the shape of women,
                finger touching finger
                hands' heels joined,

a dark look in, funnelling the dark of the hand's flesh
to a chink of lozenged light,

                                a hole that is from joining,
& to which we hasten
                over the deserts of the hand, to breathe.

A Fable

once was a woman
showed her
self
all through the psyche
of the town,
her hairy
lipped sisters
particularized
Eros:
"watch
out for serpent
Love
        dont waste your
time you
hear me on
him"

        so the woman
long past
her girlhood
looked in the night
on naked Love

who stirred in the
light, said

"wont you ever
let my trust
go on sleeping
in the dark
of our mutual
intentions,
turn off the light
& dont look at me
with the eyes of the
town in your eyes"

so she went
back & told her
sisters "it
happened just
like you wanted
he looked at me
& saw you
looked at me
& saw for the
first time
the whole
stinking family
the whole
town what
will I do
now I am
vanished
into everything
else"

& they laughed
& brought out wine
in slender

corinthian jars
& they said

"it will not
make any
difference
after a while

if a man
really loves
a woman
he will take
the sour
with the sweet
& will respect
her connections
& the society
from which she rose"
& they drank
wine & gave some
to Psyche

who went home
drunk & said to
Eros "I am
not a woman
I am your Wife
use me
after the intricate
customs of your
secrecy

& let me shine
in the darkness
of what you are"

but Eros said
"we have lived
here too long
even the rocks
are the town's
rocks & the trees
drink poison
from the shadows
of the townfolk
on their roots
we must build
a labyrinth
to hide the monster
of our perfected
love"

& Love
hid themselves
in his city.

from The Book of the Running Woman

Hagar, the rejected, the sent,
sent with her child without water & food
bare thorn bush, to gnaw sad branches

      Now the angel of the Lord declared a well
in the Desert
           (Deseret—we are in body, we are any
body, dream of Texas, cottonwoods by the branch,
offering a self beneath each one, a taste & no more,
offering my gasoline romance, my cash, car spent in desert,
roads, intercourse
               your hips how we
fled from things, your body twisted at stairtop)

            Hagar! Flight
into nowhere from the Long Island parkways,
into nowhere from the Bronx street,
Shaker Heights train into nowhere,
into the cities which are not,
              flight
where I cannot follow, where no child I make
stands at my knee
          (in the last avenues of morphine I found you,
came to you in the spiritual places where you & your sisters
kept a Grail filled with honey

                filled a pen for me with natural ink
& held my hand while I wrote your American histories
cold windows & red sumac,
                    sugar maple brittle as gold)

woman of flight & rooms of a house,
                        woman, house you are,
rooms of you,
                Hagar, the Rejected, the Fled into Desert
(room after room of the endless world)
                      mother of no one,
mother of red seed & white egg,
                  mother of black sand & sulfur spring,
mother of alkali meadows,
                woman. But the Lord
opened a well in the desert,
                your child drank your breast,
drank your blood when the breast dried,
                    Hagar,
the thorn you tore your breast with, Hagar, for him who also
leaves you, even he,
                even the conglomerate stone
rolled from your hand.
                Hagar, the car was empty,
the face at the steering wheel no face,
                  the man you kissed
was fertile of nowhere.
                The song of Hagar
in the broken foursquare temple, altar of alkali,
at the gate of despair:

                Did I not serve your power,
                emptying lord
                of a half-lidded eye,

did I not bear your unmeaning
to you again in the wordless child?
Why do you drive me away
to a land without water

where even that fruit falls away
untasted from my mouth
that starts from your limestone thighs?

Measurement of his face) Hagar saw
the broken kilometers of God's jaw,

the earnest millstones of his face, howl
of hypocrites snorted from his nose, her soul

understood the interrupted journeys of his eyes,
knew the foreshortened forehead, amber hair,

Hagar carried

nowhere in her side

Part Two: The Rose Garden of the Magician

enough of roses)
                    The columns ascend
& with their faces
                    protract
the closing circle of,
                    enough of roses!
What .
        is the name of this time?

rose time . thorn time . red time

       soft
(enough of roses!) flower, will we
ever have
       (enough of roses)
the cross
       borne for us from the beginning

the crucifixion in the rose's heart
the cross-eyed fiction only
            we come to at the end of our noses,
wise men of Sodom
           to sea in their salt
washed their weeping away,
         first
material light of seed & thorn & roses
(enough of roses)
        I yoked my eyes
followed my nose
       saw & wept
dry the place I came to.
         The prince
reposed, said "Enough of roses!
Bring me ices, & spiced wines,
          spiked wines & sure bets,
let those dance
      who'll dance to me of more than roses
let me be in their body's journey
         past all . inversion"
(through separation,
       petals full, tread light
  hips examined by thorns, plucked
a lively satisfaction,

                        separation)
                                    "dance" (Scheidekunst)
        "dance"
                (the separations, scheide diese Liebe)
                                            "dance
them for me who dance beyond desires,
rub against the painted columns
& smear with their exertions
                            the faded roses of wise instruction."

So the prince reposed.
                    Morning.
And evening aromatic as the moon
entered the magician's body:

wake to this dance you called for,
this is the president's cotillion,
quadrille of the christmas wolf,
pavane of lost occasions,
                        leap
the galliard of unlikely pleasures,
do not touch the book.
                    Tame the flame.
("I see too much," the Prince complained.)

"Take these dance away."
                        Gone, they leave
nothing behind. Ritual inversion.
The Prince sleeps. All night the magus
tends the disembowelled fires,
nibbles the flame.
                Far am I Lord away
            heal me with these flickerings heal
            with flame & over-narrated rose

Far as I am I am no place.

An die ferne Geliebte

Ea — Enki — Enlil

  air over sea over

who is that rapt figure on the white throne
gesturing
back into the western lands, the cycle?

the world
was ever a garden

(& Williams knew that, had to abide
the unrich nerve-sick lives gave
images for poetry,
that the beauty is *in* the anguish
chosen, not the evasion of,

even if it meant letting the wife know
you're doing it with
                             every
no, not every
            one.

                    Male is Odd.
Ea on air, we live on

(what comes through)
                    air,
Enki, whose sea he said was garden,

Enlil he never knew until you stood
                    before that throne
          Osiris said : Tend *my* garden.

Ea, fruitfly on my table.
No, the song was above the anguish or only about it,
     was Pindaric, sang of the exceptional,
     found triumph,
     found no triumph in the vanquished,

but no one is beautiful who cannot talk to me
                    no matter what mouth
what
"merciless
beauty"

& so it is on July 4th the inhabitants of Annandale
march up the road in cool sun
a fife a drum a plastic kazoo
a starter's pistol, a Union Jack
held by an elegant man, an american

early american, flag, by a girl, flag,

Ea the fife, Enki the drum, Enlil the flag
of the western sky filled with dying stars
                    stars being born
suns returning to their places & the world begins again
Annuit coeptis novus ordo seclorum

                              fruit fly
graceful on air,
                   a marching band
        ten men & two women, one
in tight white jeans,
                      our eyes on her
        following the imperious globes,
                              the yardstick proper;
potent, addressed.

                   Fruitfly, what is sweet
                   is everywhere, is here,
& all the beautiful women I will never touch
do not diminish me,
                   fruitfly.
Or themselves. Secure, apart, each thing, itself, apart,
the ends of the world held
                         firmly in mind. Fruitfly,
have you been loved?
                   Apostrophe to a bug.
Ea holds you in his air,
Osiris lets the drum continue
marking our time, we march
back to the biosphere

O beautiful star women distant belovéd
open your robe away
                   open
        on the other side
where life abstains from chemical

where your poets
        enter an *absolute* mystery of death
& leave no wisdom

(Oedipus, family man, homme sérieux, anständiger Mensch, gimp,
Oedipus cannot heal even the bickering of his children
                                            but walks
into mystery & the ground trembles; he is unseen a blessing on
the land, a Moses who made it, absolute fact of his

                    penetrating

leaving no story behind beyond
                            he was here, he is not anymore.

But the sun on Annandale is beautiful,
maple & ailanthus shade my house,
the girl plays up the road
                        she
filled her clothes, made music,
insane with dialectic,
                    who cares, fruitfly
        through the smallest mesh of screen
enter my house unwelcome
unseen, hover,
                taste a sweetness
                        I cannot imagine
                on the orange peel, the brown slipped
                        skin of the banana,
in *our* dark,
                taking death bravely, my hamfist waved
or my pressed thumb,
                        knowing no other garden
                than here where death mows the lawn,
the smell of cut grass sweet on the evening air.

A Constant Telling of the Father and His Widdershins

                      who arose
from his sweaty footprint
on the palace floor
he was on his way
to the caressive maidens of the bath
who folded the waters on him
each Friday night
his cup
he sat in the water
his cup was full

but from the footprint embryoed three sons
who turned all day against their father

linked? lucked together
by this common rousal
                    ("who
is our mother?") for a long
time they asked)
                      or did his footprint
belong to earth
tracks in the yard
twixt hall & bath-house?

the girls splash & the young sons

crowd at the cracks in the wall
"that is our father"
"which?"
"among the waters"
"who?"
"himself among the women"
"waters"

●

now when the queen their father's wife
saw these independents
jowling their way through her hallways
she called to her gossip, Mary she said

these are the autochthoni
the Bishop of Gissop warned us of,
the full-faced carriers of the king's genetics
up to no good
                    Sweep them out
or have old women sweep them out
we, we are not old

●

the children heard but were they children—
"I fear the touch of those ancient women
or the older ones still they threaten"
"our father's wife is thirty if a day,
look at the track of moons athwart her face
the moistness in her middle she
covers with her hands"
                    "no hands like hers
should ever touch us, our father has different hands"

(careening screaming the dry old women came
whapping their brooms down in every corner)

"they come, now
we are antipodes"
the sons run
against the sun
"for our tender lives
against the sun,
run, ostensible brothers, run"

they reached the throne's room
& heard behind the shuddering of the brooms
The king had a long cigar
a fleck of soap dry on his left ear—
Who are you
who run against my currents
& baffle my wife's hallways
turning dark to light
& blurring light with your whirring movement?

"we are your sons
or sons of your presence
or names that rose
when you passed our way,
last Friday, near the dead birch tree,
between your bedroom
& the bath-house door,
about 11:30, no moon"

Alas, you are my occident
said the king, No place
for any of us to hide

(at the door the old women
shuffled respectfully
come to free him
from his excessive sons)

•

the king was stymied—
I hardly know you
you claim some kinship with the earth
some sky above you, part of it is me
Explain to me
with the fire of youthful logic
why I should befriend you
why is what I'm asking, why

"you went among those bath-house girls
they cleaned your memory & oiled your hair"
"you dont remember the birch tree
the footstep of your left foot—
your right foot held in air
where could it go, had to go down
touch earth, make us, made us
we are made"

the king went bleary
behind his cigar
knew it was important
but it had happened before
—What happens only once is sad
he said Get out of my comfortable room

"from every step we arise & arise"
"save us from the abolishing women"

"we are not like you, there is no
space in us for smoke & fire"

even while they spoke they danced around him
& he knew their fate
You are linked to each other
go do it that way
range outside my house
turn the earth away from me
I love no earth
I love the virgin & inconsequent
I loathe my bearing & her bringing forth
get out of my intelligible room

•

turned left at the doorway
down a secret stairs
the sons ran
              (the old
women snuffled after them
blind in the dark building)

"we are beyond the light"
"we have transcended our enemy"
"we are outside where there is no building"
"we're linked with luck"
"we turn"
"we turn"

no one now followed
there were three of them
& it was night again

now they were one day old

"it profits us to run
we are the children of the king
his footsteps
we follow in ourselves, we follow"

all around the night

•

when they were two days old cast lots:
"there are three of us & must be two"
"use crow feathers"
"choose"
the center held short feather:
"call on my mother to turn me to stone"
"who is our mother"
"call stone to be stone"
"stone stone"
the middle brother was stone
they danced around him
"only for a time be stone
only for a time our dance"

the middle brother danced where he was
the other two danced the ends of the earth
"this is my end"
"this is my end"
"when we're seven days old
we'll kill our father"

•

was the father even alive to be dead—
that is the question their answer crowds

on the third day were the ends of the earth
turned
from west to east, asked
"is our father risen?"

where he sat the smoke
of his cigar obscured the maidens

I had a dream, wife,
let me tell you my dream
The queen
did not want his used-up dream
said This is my morning
too early for you to smoke
or blur my possibles
Go to the bath & talk
to the waters
or the water's daughters
taking their care

—But I had three sons
Am & Isnt & Where
Has & Ham & Hant
North & South & Between
I had three sons
by no woman
they went
their own ways I feel
them up to some mischief
everywhere

Dream your own dreams—
for me the fumes
of hot chocolate,
Why
did I marry an old all-day-long
when I could have married the morning?
Think of your legitimates
not these vestiges, these ingrate isolations
Our sons bring their daughters
come in cars & tell us they love us
when did these sons of yours ever
care enough to tell us lies?

—Already you've banished them
you & your active old women
whatever they would have meant
they wont mean now

Let them wear themselves out with their turning!

•

it took time to turn

"we own a spirit that they disdain"
"how many days till we kill our father?"
"our luck
allows waiting"
"will he be changed?"
"I said to our brother the stone:
You are our mother
He answered
Am my own mother"
"if we are who we are

what need do we have of mothers"
"turn against our father
dont let him rest in one place"

•

they came to the palace shaped like fire
"we cant even mean what we mean"
"despise the genesis that casts us out"

no door would close
no milk
lingered unsoured in the pitcher
no dust in the sunbeams
every wind
terrified of windows
the house
was still
they came
on their father as he heard music

"we have changed the poles of your music
we have broken the field of the earth
now will you hear us?"
"I make myself into notes of music
my brother is the interval
my brother is the silence you call rest"

"we take the billowing air from this room
abrogate your atmosphere—
no sound in this vacuum"
they were hidden in music & the music hid
their father gaped like a fish
breathed the deepest air inside him

died
rose in impossible airless fire
fled gasping across the world
feeding the fire he was with the lingering music inside him

"come" said the brothers
"we will run to meet him
run to meet father
over the empty rim of the world

run to meet father, run east
we'll hurry east & you
stone
wait for him here"

from The Pastorals: Section 2

An elevation. The Greeks were happy
with erectile tissue, conceived their joy
connected with that uprising. We want
the whole body to erect, body politic,
we want a revolution, a social erection

to fuck the obscurity of life on earth,
to burn up money. This was the intention
of pastoral, ice-cream cone for a penny,
free newspapers, a flute made from grasses,
a looking-glass lake. Sun, moon,

& suchlike continuities. Alexandria
was cluttered & hot, passions began
(for the first time?) to compete with money
—not very successfully. So there had to be a place
where Desire could win hands down, wallets

only to put phone numbers in, free wine, free eats
& You available in the landscape.
That was Arcadia, a false remembrance
of the time before money, a 52 week vacation
from a 52 week perversion of work (love) work.

Since work also rightly is passion. But who

remembers that after the Medici Bank, who cares
what work is if work leads to money?
Our dutch beginners discovered time was money,
more one made more the other, was it true?

didnt matter, seemed to be true & work
became no destination, just an equation. We pay
by the hour (week, year) & what we pay for
precisely is time degraded from the life of passion,
we pay men to keep them from Arcady.

Once it mattered what they did in that time
(so many urns turned, so many cords chopped,
so many letters written) but now we know better:
it is time itself we pay them for, to keep
them from passion & thus, thus, keep them from work.

Since work is passion, & passion being
serious about the world. Clear? Can we go back
to find the seacoast of Connecticut? No. Clean
it from money? No. This clarity (if it is)
is just beginning. We want a social erection.

from THE PASTORALS (*Book VI of The Common Shore*) (1972)

Section 3

The woman picked out a landscape by Claude
where cattle ford the skin of a stream, mirrored,
herded by a red-loinclothed boy. Fishermen
on a boat where the stream becomes a pool
inside the shadow of a sandstone castle. Very soft

sky, a tall tree with a clump of leaves, hills
far away. So much description. Trees also
grow on the battlements. 1650? More cows away,
more people, some riders. It's the big forked tree
that hangs the picture from the sky. The postcard

gives a few inches to this seen world, a few
suspicions of color, red of the boy, sepia cattle,
faint margin of blue hills. Sits above my desk
& I've never asked why she chose it. Maybe
it's the world she means us to wander in,

close to the earth & the answered question,
maybe it's the world I have to destroy. Maybe
it is Arcadia, & the castle of Queen Venus's house
or public library of love or granary of desire
or the whole thing just flickers in the sky

& I see the reflection over my desk, a landscape

she means me only a little bit to notice.
No sun in the picture. Bring sun, forgo
imagination that does not soon discern its country,
does not enter it in state & take possession.

Find the country & go in. Eat the cows, love
the herdsmen. These men work. Live the house.
But this tree becomes the linden at our house,
these cows cars, fishermen carpenters, buzzsaw
down the glen, birds sing. The sky is the same sky.

What did she mean by Claude Lorraine, by cows
& lollipop trees, cool water, light turns to sound,
too much going on, why are all the people there?
This is confusion, street-scenes after an act of passion
water idling past our failed insurrection.

Against the Code

Language is the only genetics.

        Field
"in which a man is understood & understands"
     & becomes
     what he thinks,
becomes what he says
          following the argument.

When it is written that Hermes or Thoth invented language, it
is meant that language is itself the psychopomp, who leads the
Individuality out of Eternity into the conditioned world of
Time, a world that language makes by discussing it.

So the hasty road
& path of arrow
must lead up
from language again

          & in language the work be done,
work of light,
      beyond.

Through manipulation and derangement of ordinary language
(*parole*), the conditioned world is changed, weakened in its

associative links, its power to hold an unconscious world-view (consensus) together. Eternity, which is always there, looms beyond the grid of speech.

Elgar's Second Symphony

A patchwork quilt
in old countries,

shame for a man
to have no religion.

The lime tree?
                    Morning
over the hill
when grey
is a primary color?

Repeat the way the sparrow does,
variation & dance, nothing big.

Patchwork—
homespun is fashionable
if you can get it.
They drive out here
on the Lord's day,
we bong the chapel bell
to make them think god.

•

Winter apples of Annandale
lie back of the road,
                              deer
chewed them, snow quilted them over,
now snow leaves them alone.
Spring starts this month
all over again.

•

Even in these fields
I walked with him.
Night fell.

All the owls
understood the thermometer.

Theater of a critical surgery,
this quarter-acre
the last footstep in Eden.

•

This music moves me more than I can say.
If I were suspicious I'd think about that.

But it *is* here, & what I hear
is beautiful. I go along with it

trusting, its big soft floppy heart
companionable, traveling.

                              Freedom
just past that locust tree.

•

Edom. When it sounded like this
all the time. When the vicar
still wore horns & the choros
of naked girls circled
widdershins around the church,

circled around me & I
married every one of them, every one,

& a voice from the earth cried out
I love you, my son, my last born.

The Sound

First she heard a sound
like thunder,
bright sky

or heavy armchairs
moved
on the floor above her

when she was alone in the house
so she went out
when the sun

came through mist
& walked into the shadow
of a maple on the soft road

she heard far off
a hammer in the woods
she followed it

down along the stream
to the second waterfall
there was a man

"I am building" he said

& went on hammering,
she watched the pale

groaning wood, his arm
swung from the elbow
going down

"I am the human soul"
she said
"& I heard your hammer

in my only woods"
"I am building" he said
"a house or a table,

a horse or a child,
springtime & little
flies with golden wings,

you hear the sound
of thunder from an
empty sky"

"I am an actress
in this play" she said
& there was the

thunder again
though his hands were
still now, his eyes

fixed on her,
wondering.
"I suppose

you are no one
& this hour
betrays me

now I am near
the end of my work.
Go back home

& let me settle
this strife I have
with the old wood,

the seasoned wood"
she heard him
but the thunder

was all over her mind.

In Mahler's Sleep

an archaic austerity
comes out of the ground

(bird skeleton, snake skeleton,
no redundancy)

comes out & confronts the sea.

•

& even the Cycladic vastnesses
were tricked to stand
                    unlimed,
the big rocks cut true
hang true;
            courses of specific gravity,
each rock remembers
the kernel at the center of the earth,

is loyal to that energy. Affinity.

•

The sack that holds the sandman's sleep
is stitched of many birds, feathers still on,

beaks still on & they cry out,
                    source of the high-frequency terror
our throats try to imitate
at the gates of nightmare,
                    groan of ancient door
we struggle to keep closed.
                    Wake dry. Larynx tight.
Our waking
is the last articulation of the dream.

•

In Mahler's sleep the yellow houses
fill with wise peasants, dead sheep
hang near the ovens, summer evening
is coming, air pale, the picture

precise as a glass of wine.
                    Mice
wait outside the granary
for a saint's permission to enter & eat
                    —their whole lives this tiny hunger
never stops—

and a rabbi waking from desire
bellows out his window
an ancient cockcrow
he learned from the heart of night.

•

By the stream almost dark now
the water lilies he thought they were
turn into a woman in green silk

who sits in the shallow water.
When he sees the sunset through her
he knows he's been tricked again,

once again his only friend is far away
traveling the emperor's road, dust, blue
distance, his only friend is
far away, he wakes with the distance in mind,
it stretches out, a definite number of
some measure, he's forgotten the number
& only brings to mind the direction:
                                    the way the shadows point,
towards sunrise.

•

But morning is a crystal & a crystal is a stone.
A man lives three times longer than a hawk
but a bird can lead the man to the stone.

Trapped by the morning sky
the hawk falls out of his dream.

The austere thing is warm in his hand.

Ralegh

Caught in the window
breath of air
                    lately on the big round wood table
        under the spruce, a level
outside to work on
                    & let the air love me.
        The children of light
            summon this apparition,
church in the world . church of the world,
angel disguised as a spruce tree)

        •

                    Ralegh appears in the dusk,
his queen a lost memory:
                    "I was kinder when I loved her
& sailed to the island for her,
                    this spindle island
half as big as the world.

            Tell her for me
        the years delight to pass
        & the cool air of July
        is sweet under love's trees.

On this big roll of parchment a map of these fields,
                              thousands of miles, waters,

& on the little vellum folded in four
            my plan of the City
        we will one day begin to build her—

                the legend is in cipher
                to protect our studied proportions
                from foreign architects.

                              The stone she sent me
        casts no shadow.
                    Tell her for me
                    in love's name
                    we will go
                        on trying forever,
                    rising & falling on the sweet
                            wave of the
                            work she gave us.

Quincunx in the garden, a knot of simples
round me as I write, I smell them around me
all afternoon as I thank her for my death

& all the Last Things,
                    tansy, campion, rue, basil,
        stavesacre,
their air blows kindly through my house

where in the evening fire I see the faces
of all her lovers
dancing with her, amiable, not too fast,

& therein even her particularity
merges in all
lovers whatsoever

in that glowing white hot place
                        below the flame
in the heart of the incandescent wood
where all the images stand still."

Linguistics

I.

That stirs the way of seeing it,
vocabulary
of a poor people
                    rich in iliads,
in things & defined acts

                    perceptions of use
in the brief daylight.

Any sane man hates the cold & dark.

Mihrab.   Turn this way
(away from what you are)
pray
outside your geography.
                    The clock
will never be invented.

2.

Language of a besieged minority,
our words & theirs.

To build a house
first paint the door
blue, wall white. A box
of song birds at every door.

Greek islands. So when the killers
come to kill
you have a simple word to say
known only by those about to die.

The great secret
but you leave it to the singing birds to say.

3.

When the set is properly grounded
your receiver will pick up
light verse of the gods
& detailed instructions
sent hourly from the Great Bear.
Fang music of Mercury
is easy to get, & steady
sighs from the exasperated Moon.

The problem is Earth
& again, the problem is Earth.
Who would believe these messages
cracked on the tongue like sticks
across the knee,
                    say it & spoil it?

To hear it at all
implies the transmission is false,
property of the atmosphere to deceive.

4.

A change had happened
& a different language
poured through his throat—

"I'm home! *This*
is America, not that hot
banana continent
swarming with frightened men"

He had his hands together, loose,
& looked into the dark between them
where a little light came through
colored by his skin.
                    He watched
till stars came out
& gave them the names he loved
lifted off the map of the lost republic.

5.

A knowledge of the future
is what the close
study of written texts provides,
given a reader
wise with natural sympathy:

in some book is recorded
each thing will ever happen.

That is not style.
These words now

are part of your future
(not just that I'll be there for breakfast)

& the least song
rimes with the end of the world.

The Customs Inspector

Everything starts in the same way.
The eye grows weary
of checking where they hide their diamonds.
These amateur smugglers
put them everywhere
but mostly in the same predictable places—
in vulva or anus
armpit, shoe (how can they walk?)
perineum behind scrotum
(how can they sit down?)
in their mouths so that they mumble
in their ears so I have to shout.

They're smuggling diamonds from the East
but most of them, maybe all,
have forgotten they're doing that
& mostly think of themselves as innocent—
it's been a long trip.
Where's the diamond? What's a diamond?
that's what they tell me
yet when I look at them quietly
my eyes not accusing, just being clear
on them & at them,
they get nervous, anxious, soon reveal
where they hid the stone

or where—without even their full
conscious awareness—the stone
was hidden in them by professionals
or for all they knew
maybe it hid itself in them.

I can tell by the way they squirm
what part of their bodies it's hidden in.
And then I have to call it out,
treat them carefully
& make them discover the stone themselves.
They feel better when they find it.

I'm not supposed to touch them
but sometimes their grace or awkwardness
touches me, & I move to help,
be of help, remind them of all the places,
dark hollows of themselves.
Sometimes I reach in & touch the stone.

Eve of St. Mark's

Tonight the dust's footprint shows the about to die,
wraiths at churchdoor

                            & what we always affirm
is more of the same.
                   Maybe it is each name
we cling to that condemns us,

                               our track, our well-known
footstep in the ashes.

                       The bitterest wine
           is to be no one

                     but it cleanses & heals.

The Centerfielder

At the brink
a lovely rain
         & light
where it's coming from

I hear a sequence
rhythm
of an exact unfolding

necessary
between people like us
when I so much am
in love with substance

catch it there
in the golden outfield
far from the batter's
creative wrists

I can do nothing unless it comes down.

Love Song I

The grunion
are coming

it is complex
& predictable

they arrive
connected with the moon

men
who have lived longer
run to capture

this subtle sort of thing that
doesnt happen every night. I'm

not interested. Everything I care for
happens all the time.

from The Loom: Section 3: The Sea Machine

To look for God
look like God.
To find water in the earth
cut your dowsing fork
from one of water's trees
(hazel, willow, cottonwood)
& hold it as if backwards
turned in your hands
so that the lawfulness
of hidden water
deep below the earth
will act upon the fork
to make it flow straight
as water does
always obedient
to its one possibility.

Our loveliest jewel
is to begin anywhere.
Bay of Naples on my mind,
volcano plume, a boat
thucks across the smooth hot
water & the breeze
is what we'd rather not,
hot, & there are indolent women

160   *from* THE LOOM (1975)

wobbling on deck,
a cruise out of sight
moving (wrong time of day)
late afternoon
right into the sun.
Eyes wrinkled closed
but sweat in the furrows
thick, like the olive oil
we think of in this place.
An egg
in the palm of my hand,
dull shell, getting sweaty,
a few cracks already,
hardboiled this morning
soon to be metallic,
will I eat or let it sink
I toss it
it sinks, bobs, rises, settles.
History of an Egg in the Bay at Naples
in three volumes, octavo,
illustrated with curious views of the natives
& seven appendices
each in smaller print than the one before.
Graphs maps tables & charts.
We're moving west, slow journey
to Palma in the Balearics,
unlikely. An old man, a Christian
but wearing a turban, bends on the rail
beside me: "My name
is Ramon Lull, & men
have ceased to believe in my existence.
I invented this machine you're looking at."
—What machine?
"The sea, the cybernetic

movements of the waves
or hadnt you noticed.
Before my time, the Mediterranean
moved like any ocean,
a larger but less intelligible machine.
Pretending to be a missioner
intent on converting the Moor
I crossed it repeatedly,
way out there where we're going,
between Mallorca & Africa,
& on each crossing laid
in careful order
certain crystals & dusts of metals,
feathers & lockets & herbs
into the sea
in such a way
its rhythm, through the whole Mare Nostrum,
began to change.
Now a man who knows what he's doing
(rare!)
& who can understand the workings
of my machine
(not hard, once he realizes
that it is a machine—
that's always the problem,
isnt it, but I wander)
& who has a problem to solve
(o rarely!), why such a man
can read off his answers as he sails.
He sets his problem out
by the way he trims his sails—
he reads their shadows, reads
his own shadow. Time of Day."

from Section 9, Sonata in A♭: The Essay on Form

To listen
when it does not speak.
To determine
the exact distance
between any word & any other
& by skill to map
the landscape between.
Then coax the word to speak.
Melody
especially when it grieves
(arioso dolente)
takes your hand.
Leads you
willing or unwilling
to the pine-lit
wedding chamber,
you are married
to the fact of it,
the light goes out
on all you've felt
or failed to feel.
Grief
     is the distance
between loves
            sometimes stepwise,

sometimes reversing
its course
as when we move close
& grief is the cave
our present joy
lights up,
                        go slow,
grief is distance,
even the miles we traveled
to be together
ache under us.
Just this once
not to be caught
in statement or story,
but to flow
justly
over the contours
of your body
in the liberty of light.

Truth is a day,
& every day.
Refute that
& be wiser
than your eyes,
& sorry.
I want to take your time,
linger
is the shape of it,
an hour
is to go through.
Gate after gate.
That is what the form of words
(forming a place for words)

lets in,
      & what the Matter is
of our work,
to let the time
speak itself through.
Sometimes
we've been making love so long
we almost forget
we're doing anything,
& then an acceleration
begins in my throat
to find some word
shaped like what it is
to be me in you,
that might answer
all the subtle
information
to which your body
all this while
subjects me,
learning
while my heart & breath
hunt for the word
(it must sound like you)
& when I look at your eyes
sometimes open
the humid fire
so far below
increases
& I am urgent to say
so that from an immense distance
further than any grief
a word begins to travel
through me, I can hardly

understand it, I am not even
interested in it, it approaches,
I want to brush it away,
I will not submit
to its definition, but its will
seduces mine, it has your
name on it but
is not yet your name,
I hold you tighter now
& the word catches fire,
burns me, the smoke
conceals its sound, the fire
seems more like your fire,
there is affinity, a rime
aching to sound, its road
begins to open, my gates
burned down & nothing but
gates everywhere opening,
I know what the word must be,
its simplicity
has tricked me again,
I struggle
to resist
the ease of it,
it has come
from everywhere I am
& will not be refused,
even, there begins
to be no longer any
part of me that knows
how to refuse,
I look at your closed eyes
& know
　　　　　the precise shape

of what must come
now
      leaping to fill it
& louder than I could
ever have imagined
it suddenly speaks.

Ode 15

Direct to transpire: the Devil is;
that Delos of unreason doubts the go
hence never went. It is no copula
or any even amber light to slow.
It is a drag. No hum in Its nose
no jump in Its come. Alderman
of neglect, Negus of the mountains of No.
I spell it for you in this fishy way
to cause to coalesce one afternoon
late a privative postman full of woe
stealing words & even meanings
from the ashblond vanity where sits
an opalescent fleshy friendly honey
painting her eyelids with pale blue soot.
While she watches her self in the mirror
he gathers twelve years of lovesongs
from her hollow ears, he sucks out
her lovely memories, his fingers
trace her fears on her smooth skin
& make her think she's getting old.
Sigh. He's taught her walls all
round her. He takes the mail away.

Ode 16

That I came to know it all
fernbrake & morning glory tilted
trumpet to heaven, lust hibiscus
battering the wall. The green all
to know with my red mind full
of the rhapsodies of language bare or vested
the mere reach of this rich as-is.
Reality is escape. The rusty junk
of fervent highways soothe the mind
into self-consoling slumber. The real
real is intimate, hard to find,
locked & released at once in thought,
beyond the touch of poignant imagery.
Old men have syntactic minds.
Here winter is stored against delusive
solstice calms & small pink flowers.
Against deceitful resurrections.
This time does not come again.

The Lady Of

To the Reader

"The Lady Of" is a reconstitution of an ur-*The Lady of Shalott*, and means to rescue a doctrine of woman from that curiously empty, frightening, beautiful old poem

(its absence clogged with memories, the colors of distance and gone and loss, colors all saturated by the polarizing filter of Tennyson's rhetoric).

Like a crumbled frieze whose figures are lost but whose proportions are still evident, *The Lady of Shalott* casts a certain work-space in the mind, a shapely shape.

(How shapely the original is! How its shape is lovelier than its logic, if that could be. (It can't be.) How the shapely waist of the poem pinches the middle of the story until we lose what really happened, and are left only with her loneliness. I mean loveliness. Loneliness. Loveliness. Loneliness. How did she die? Of her own beauty? Is that the "curse" Tennyson speaks of, a fated perfection of line and color, ominous as Psyche's beauty?)

The original casts a shapely proportion in the mind the moment now comes to inhabit and to articulate anew.

1.

She woke & found her city was besieged by her.
But it all was light, dazzling around her from
the little windows, ribbon-glass of Roman bowls
set up on windowsills above her stream.
No way to go on living there. Potency of glass.
She'll let the boat loose down she sits in
coming to Camelot. I let her flow.

2.

Still near the graham dust under begonias,
small moist domes of her hortensias
known here elsewise under the window.
Indoor-outdoor carpet they step up
to move past the lemonade come calling,
bringing lilacs in their hands for her, their seasons,
to remember the cool breath pooled
this moment down there in the flowers.

3.

She was red in the boat & remembered.
Arid reach of almost water she would have thought
had she been, a small phial or cordial
she had brewed under a happier less
conscious sun once.

4.

Chanted the spirit of yesterday.
Alarming, jewels along her arm,
sards & onyxes at finger ends
etudes, mazurkas, emeralds, pearls.
She flows in her clothes I marvel.
Who look on. Who is good to look on.

5.

The sliced tomatoes rest in the sun.
All women are lovely, or is it sunshine
passing through the mason jars full of prunes,
green faint blue of the grass. Last
night spring water boiled was poured upon them.

6.

And nearer to the king, through the curtained light
the plain linen runner on the piano,
this chinese bowl, bourgeois translucency.
Whenever the word "king" appears the song goes wrong.
She floats in the bizarre intention
that, rising briefly from the not dustless sofa,
flecks around her in sunlight defining where she went.

7.

She sings on an ivory scale, her alphabet
is peaches with pears, or she decides to change

into animals that chase each other small
in & out of pickerel weed beside so slow a stream
they play. Her discourse twists inside out.
Sad to see such a lovely woman pass
into this mysterious suicide outside of town.
Glad, that women turn from society
into the magic solitude of their crystal difference.
Sad when they pay for it. The car
fills with exhaust fumes by the lake.

8.

It is of swans who also mutely perish
falling through the air of folklore to a silent lake.
Theme of the woman alone, her joy, loss, lake.
It is beast around her at the first white-water—
I saw the hungry otters rise, hazelnuts fall.
Then they were shadows I thought, the river
as if at Stockbridge, deep pools & shallows.
They were shadows.

9.

"Love as an idea is a product of objective practice."
Which had a lot to do with the fig trees bare at that season
& hens being slaughtered on the rocks, sacrifice, men
walking separate from women, not even fighting,
building, not killing. A dream, but not her dream yet.
When will the strife be over she thought but
she thought it would never be over, because the boat,
because the swans, because the trout
could never make common cause with fishermen.

10.

And that was the slaughter of being alone,
to see all those fields & hillocks now
she was leaving them forever.
She thought of her lover
that difficult flower
as she imagined him on the castle wall,
a pawn she realized now in the class struggle.
That it all is a struggle & nothing isnt,
& the struggle defines everything
even the feel of water on the heel of her hand
she trails from the listless boat.
That she would let her hand drift.
That she would drift.

11.

That "love is a product" was shocking enough,
when all her dominies had called it Cause,
a sort of metaphysical Poet of vast occasions
ardent in the sky like Helios but never setting.
And it may be that too, she guessed,
but it can only come amongst us a product,
fruit of what we do.
It was nice to think of growing things,
of chinese parsley, of coiled
caterpillars waiting for their cues.
Of him too up on the battlements.
And she knew all at once it was love that was killing her.

12.

The electric blender of lunch-time salads
was grinding near the air conditioner
& the two sounds together asserted a pastoral
promise that she, living, could take
healthy things into her body.
Then the sound set a yellow tablecloth
& put down a white piece of cheese
in the brief midnight between morning & evening, this noon.
Were they thrips on the gloxinias, the tiny things?
She had heard the word, & it was spring.

13.

O all those words we hear
that come back in the morning to bite us!
Disease is that way, the mountain
outside the reform-school window is that way,
the details of wildlife in magazines
or capitals of small republics.
That is, they haunt. They are like food.
They are food.

14.

So the canoe drifted from the region of her purity
(which is puberty) into the glades of perhaps
& at last into the iron-gated Brunel tunnel
which took the canal under Mount Doubt
& let it out beyond. She saw the gates
& they made her think about her girlhood,

how intense she was then. And she understood
that innocence is not lost by sexuality
but is itself lost when sex intensity is lost.
Innocence is being in the world & wanting more.

15.

Women are terribly vulnerable to what they hear about men
& she had heard about this one,
thin single image of compassionate hauteur
before whose sturdy not-quite-comprehension
she could run herself aground, or float past him
into the permanent discontinuity of the sea.
Suffer for him, die for him to see her do so.
For no more reason than she heard of him.

16.

Is this the story of a soul getting rid of itself?
There were nineteen at the start, stanzas, measure
of years in the Judean cycle, how Lady Sun
relaxes down the decades until one day
she hears herself called "him" & loses touch
with radiant energy. The attic. And begin again.
There is a stream flows through a given house
o rapture of architecture, o driven light.
It was the building seen itself through all its furniture,
the shape below the shadows she saw from the boat.

17.

O high ambiguity to see from the stream.
Bryony to think of white she rode through willow
ease her fever.
She is a heat to get there, an all-her-life
babbling of water & fire, she'll say anything,
she has to reach out to be touched by him,
he has to do it, he must do it himself—
that much at last is clear.
My love is summery & warm & strong & he.

18.

By the sheer love she felt him, & any news was bad.
I think she didnt want him out there in the world.
All her colored threads, red of arteries blue of vein,
oranges, earth green: tangled weeks beneath her,
swans encumbered her interstitial waters.
Periscopes lifted from the wavering colors
to aim her home, welcome to herself at last,
this smashed paintbox, this grandiose Turner seascape
painted by her fear or was it her desire?

19.

I love war. They take aim to caress her
into the glad silence of being nobody.
She followed her fancy to this bright place
for the sake of the colors, colors
were her only children & all she has left.
But it was also love she summered of,

& did not forget that no men give it,
only recall it, only
bounce it off their pale tall walls.
Where he stood now watching her solution.

The Tears of Edmund Burke

Let the ink
run out & return
it is a tide
also
    like the white of its kind,

colorless energy
cloaked in sky,
a queen
on the guillotine
shimmering diamonds

        blade
    of all her falls

glistening in the wet ink.

We fix on Edmund Burke
who saw the young queen
full of beauty & wit,
loved her
as his soul
divided from him by the long
water, the Channel,
the sleeve.

And worshipped her
in tides of ink
so that men said
His politics are amours, his politics are mad,
    he has believed his own words
    & stands dazzled by the diamonds of the Queen
    reflected in his wet ink
white paper
where on sunny days
the prism
throws its manifest,

Burke wept
that his hand was so far from his head,

that his eye was so far from the ink
    & the sleeve on his wrist
would blur the letters when he wrote so fast.

Across the Channel the queen knelt
& lost her head,
diamonds tumbled down & her eyes
reflected light,
Burke could do nothing, his hand
so far from his head.
With the fire of his rhetoric
he heated the forge of his heart,
wept his fluent tears
& formed a crystal of political fact,

    Revolution kills the Woman

he thought, & that is all it does.
"It is the revenge

of men against
all beauty that moved them,
   against words & diamonds
      that made them dance

& they will no longer.
I am the last man
who saw the Queen
dance in her vigor & truth & loveliness,
the flame of her diamonds was harder than Reason

& I have worshipped it
·until the end."
He tore his roots up from the earth
& followed her
before the glisten had dried off the ink.

The Last Religion

and the pier
widened
so that the Dead
in all their difference
could board
that single boat.

Chastity

is a love of not being misunderstood,

of people at some distance,
                a "girdle"
   to preserve,
        a wall enclosing.
Freemason. The wall that walks.
   (And becomes fatuous, as in A Midsommer nights Dreame,
      only when it talks about its hole)

(we have been much too much in holes
   involved with or pursuing, in,)

this wall I will, this garden I am, that moves
   among you, moves by thinking itself there.

Rose is a Hole turned inside out.

On wet black wood Pound saw her petals
   & talked about something else for sixty years
until the acorn opened,
              clearly, in the sense of Light
& the knowledge
          that light is not vague, is a Defined,

Enclosure)
      a person)
The two Rosie+Crosses:

the Stavros crowned with seven roses,

the Crucifixion in the Rose.

A My Name

When we were children, the girls sang a counting game and jump-rope game chant:

A my name is Alice / my husband's name is Andrew /
we come from Alabama / and we sell apricots.

Tremendous stress on the last word, APRIcots. And so on through the alphabet. It was to be seen how far she could go, always and instantly coming up with a new name, a new husband, a new homeland, a new commodity, all alliterating. So our ears were trained in rhythm, how to fit the names in of different lengths, a living demonstration of the vitality of Measure and the impuissance of meter, that trivial mitre-box. Cradle of surrealism: any alliterating name would work, but only the wilder or dirtier or more wonderful ones elicited a ripple of delight from the girls standing around waiting their turn, from the boys clustering close, to hear and see all they could of this mystery.

The game chant taught this: that reality is polar, male-female, tantric. That to be entitled to be at all, you needed a wife (a husband). That you are defined by your place. That you've got to have some product, the stranger the better. That the product should have some affinity with your identity. That you've got to bring it all to market. That it all has to come to market.

This chant was my first news of the Great Trade Route along which scarce and isolate merchant-poet-nomads carried goods from tribe to tribe, over the mountains and under the sun, bringing the only news.

The Origin of It

(from a third century papyrus)

From an oak took bright
    and warmed it in the sun
    evidently honey, work of the dewloving bee
        wove all day around the god's head
    and filled the hollow of the tree
        with its intricate work
                now the sun
    broke down the obsessive cells
    to make the honey, natural from outside this
System
        flow like oil,
              and the wax flowed too
      so Pan
    his hairy arms by now all sticky
could glue his reeds together with wax
           held when cool, evening,
      his pipes
    lined up from long to short
        skyline
      of a city he had founded
    receding infinitely from his touch
           to the last lipped note
when later he tried it;

and like the bee around him danced
one other industrious feminine
a Bacche girl, she pranced
all round him
wanted his tune in her mouth,
may have meant to steal it
to dance her dances with
and Pan
touched it not too gentle to
just the edges of her lips
she blew
and he recovered his instrument
with his own mouth
and breathed into it with power or skill
such that his body
stiffened with the effort
and the muscles of his torso tensed
as only the sound poured
out and down
frightening the girl a little
then the sound
hung in her ears as she
rushed to the place of her proper dance
and later,
remembered,
was music.

The Acquisition

I saw the web resplendent strung
in the crotch of a prostrate baytree
so what little sunlight filtered down
through redwoods found its way here,
to be proclaimed & multiplied on the strands
moulded by a small body, its house & instrument.
As a brave American I tried to possess it,
doing deft things with my camera
& duly months later had the stigmata
on a nearby wall: spiderweb slung
in almost perfect focus, a glimmering
pond of standing water just behind.
Several angles, good shots, I forgot
the spiderweb & its business with the light,
I had collected an experience.
I had shared the spider's feast.

Now today in the first warmth of June
I haul this memory out, delicate, damaged
by two years in the generalizing mind
& try to reconstitute it between me
& the powdery sky. No such gothic lights,
an altogether gentler condition than California.
And by the calmness of the air I find myself
compelled to understand this web afresh

as evidence of the self's power to cast
its thought as physics in a physical world,
spin matter & consent to live in it.
But I am unfair to the spider, who has the power
to leave this cloth she's spun, resorb
her productions in her self again & travel
along straight lines difficult for us to credit
across the light & find another intersection
waiting at the end of herself for her to become.

Les Joueurs de Foot-Ball, 1908

(*H. Rousseau*)

Athletes come running up a field
held between tall trees.
The luminous ball
rises from hands or falls.

Most of the trees are lanced
with long elliptical cunnic holes.
The foliage is yellow
while the athletes hurry by.

My father is eight years old.
In nine years his brother Simon
will walk down this same glade.
There will be no flowers on the trees.

The young men who had been playing
have been eaten up by iron spheroids,
rhombic tanks, airplanes huzzahing
down on them like tantaluses

full of gallant agony. As Simon goes
a landmist of poison drifts to meet him.
Seeing it, for a moment he believes

the gas is soft blossoms on the trees,

the way they look now at evening,
corporeal light drifting through branches,
mustachioed young athletes moving towards me,
my father eight years old peers out from where he hides.

It might have been that he was near death.

Certainly foreign languages became
easier to understand.

One day he felt, looking at the Greek
text of the Iliad,

that he could in fact read there
about fires burning around a war,

about stars brittle in the sky
jiving under a fine full moon.

It was some consolation,
like Mahler, or riding a bicycle.

Then he could understand
even when people werent talking

& one day admired a shapely young
woman getting out of a car

& was suddenly overcome with her grief
even before he saw the sick

little girl she helped out, & the bleak
doctor's doorway beyond the Plymouth.

Her shape told me she was sad,
he thought, & then he allowed his thought

to make love to her & her sadness both
while he drove up the highway towards

it *must* be death it is so empty & so kind.

from "Orpheus"

3: *[He speaks to Eurydice, and is answered]*

I yield my freedom
to have known you,

you lady dim
in the interstices
of a lost network
leading out of time,

old radio broadcasts
back from the nebulae
back from the
Moon, Lady
            vague
as the moon
must be understood
to have been before
an outpost
of our entropy,

                Lady
integrable
with my needs I abash
before the selfish

will of my will,
my vajra vigor
claims you, my
songs understand you—

"Them?
I have heard
those programs before,
baked in sunday childhood boring
as before,
nonetheless I rise to you
along the Avenues of Dogs
the clement ever clement
weather of late Hell
to attend your
noises,
                    never
hope to see me

as I am."

from The Book of Persephone: Section 3
(Aria of Plutone)

"I had been walking
& the day was different
only in that I felt my body
more than usual, slip
of my thighs at times
against each other as I squeezed
between two thornbushes
or edged along red roses.
I felt sun warm my back.
The ground was soft, ill-drained
& rich lush greens came up there,
ramsons & wild chives, lilac-
flowereted alliums. Then broad & wide
where sunlight was steadier,
between two great trees, a sward
blue-starred with bright squills,
tiny flowers, the seed of summer sky
fallen here now speaking.
I understood the day
as well as I was able,
sense of my body helping to hold.

I saw the girl then, bent down to recover
one of those dark blue flowers herself—

half aloud she was asking Do they
after all have white centers, white
or pale yellow deep in the heart?
The grace of her bending low
to serve her intellectual desire
gave me such pleasure that I took hold.
Constrained by my travel she came along
willing unwilling, who can say,
still speaking softly to the flower
till she came to my House."

Section 10

Earth is a woman who imagines us. She sings
to us her different children, spider, sparrow, bear.
We are hers but she's no mother. More mint
than chamomile, more leek than affable. Free!

Syringa! I lift my glad palm to shade a name,
a new known in the jungle of vocabulary.
I call after it Come see Come be seen You
fragrant in the middle noon, heartless flower

all loveliness is civilized; I heard Bruckner
at the door; the gardener releases Merlin
from love's impetuous stone. Crush crack, noise
of rusty bedsprings being fucked on. Hark! he speaks:

"I chose my cantilenar prison, I chose my gloom.
Deep in the Forest of How-wise-I-am I let her
& she caught me as I wished; we felt each other
skin by skin, then I let her lose me down the steps.

Down in the copper-mesh Faraday chamber snug
all the mortal radio was scrambled out. Blocked,
it left me free to ultimate telepathy—
I hear the whole world thought by thought.

It is as if a tree. I have everything but distance.
And as for her, I know her every synapse in her head—
the only thing I ever loved her for at all.
For I was an old man, in love with difference."

from THE BOOK OF PERSEPHONE (1978)

Section 16 (Fourth Ode to Persephone)

The kind of rose she wants called John F Kennedy
I think of a green rose with bullet holes in its head
but she means shape, the shape the way it holds bud
taut contract against the ordinary splay "but
its color is all wrong" and what is a rose itself
but a muscle of color? lips of fragrant light?

∾

The birds told me
some
by going some by staying

Texts: 23

The bird that hovers
over the text,
      a falcon
     motionless
         above the man,
"to hover in one place,
like a hummingbird"

"by their ability"
falcons . Saka
         of the sun
        that hovers over the page
reading the world.

So one reads the page until the image comes,
moons of Granada
drenched in smooth fountains
while the bird hovers
over the chosen word.

How to read.
How to bare it, how to bear
that those smooth thighs and hips
are sometimes: wet from the fountain spray
or drenched with moons

swimming at midnight
                    or sometimes dry
                    in the choked night,
how to live
a day or a year
picking out what matters.

How to live
under the shadow
of the bird that picks me out

under the carpet.
Sweep the pattern of the carpet under the carpet
where the pattern can sink through
& become the floor.
To walk on the floor then
is to accept the condition of my effort.
I walk on my effort.
To read is to walk

again I said, Arise
& know the water
for the first time,
                    arise, the text
is open.
To wait all that while
to 'find' an image
those amorous tissues of the night
around the fountain,
women, moons, women
& to wait
all that while for an image & not
be able to live,
not live with that memory

pouring forward
where the moon
awakens
      above the cloud-band on the rim of the carpet,
the fountain sloshes over,
                the sky
         suddenly trapped on the floor.
And put that in a text.
To trap the moon in a carpet.
To unremember.
To trap the moon in a puddle on marble.
To have made the effort,
to walk through the image
to swim in the moon.
To have made the ground
               & not submitted to it.
To hover over the text.
To read.

The Long March

My father made me begin thinking in the body of my mother
on Christmas night 1934
when the First Route Army
was between Pienchai and Wengkulung.

While the army crossed mountains and rivers and deserts
and rivers again and rivers and rivers
for eight thousand miles
my mother carried me patiently

answering every question of my nature
as it searched inside her
for the tools and weapons and strategies it would need.

Even after the terrible empty grassland in the north
wadded under grey clouds went on forever
she went on

till in the heat of September
in the border regions between Kansu and Shensi
after nine months she lay down
and for three days writhed
to say me most exactly into the world,
to suffer in her body this sign of being accurate

and I came into the breath
while the exhausted heroes of the great deliverance
trudged the eleven conscious miles between Luching and
    Hsin-ssu.

A Woman from Connaught

My great-great-great-great-grandmother
on my father's father's father's mother's side
I remember with the curious vividness of all creatures.
She was small
and her perfectly round eyes had not yet
been lost in the big green slit-eyed lewdness of the Kelly eyes.
She travelled once in her long life down
from the north and west where her fathers
had been kings, and their wives and mothers
innocent harlots of sunshine,
paid by green life for all their travail,
wild sex of white-thighed women till she came along.

The exploits stopped then.
A long smouldering
match had reached at last her philosophic powder.
She exploded into a restless stillness,
read books in four languages, wore her round
eyes milky with cataract but still,
even at the last of things, thought she could see
the devoted moon go up
over the rafters of her slatternly house,
all dim spiders and dirt floors she guessed.
But the floors were good oak parquet
and her own bees made the wax that gleamed

high over her mind in the white rooms.

Their echo I still hear, rooms or bees,
song of their summing
all the names and numbers of the flowers
that writhed unseen in her garden. She was not sexy.
She thought things into place and held them there.
She could hardly tell if the candles were lit.

The skirts of her redingote trailed
at times across her feet. She thought them rats
and marvelled at their boldness,
wondered should she not be firmer with the servants,
if indeed those english-speaking shadows
were her servants, not mere ghosts
of all her enemies come back to mock
with unclear whispers at the edge of rooms.

The fields are always blank, she thought,
and autumn rebukes the summer's brashness.
It is empty. They are empty.
So blank there had to be a force somewhere
austere and honest. She called it God
and thought men ought to honor it
by books in many languages, and keeping still,
and sitting in large rooms alone.
                              Oh God
she prayed, keep the smell of the stables away.
Dont let me hear the wasps yawning all spring long.
Dont let me hear the children singing
or Sarah's petticoat slither on wet grass.
Let me know you in an Irish silence,
sweet dumb heart & clever-mouth & loving.
Let there be nothing but love and then not even that.

But when the gardener mowed the lawns
the smell of the grass came
in the long windows and stood in the room like kings.
From her I have my love of cloudy days,
long pauses in the conversation, silences
at the ends of lines of poetry, thick symphonies,
quiet women and their heavy gods.

Studies from the Mishnah: III

(DBR)

Behind
this book
I want to get behind
this book this thick
thing this afterlude
this thick belated thing this thick
this book
       I want
to get behind this book this thick
thing spoken,
           back
to the Oral Law
they say came before
& talks behind this book.
But *they say* it only in a book, this thick
replacement for a savage breath
or lover's idle soft breathing left
a minute later still ringing in the ear
how soft she said
          whatever it was she said—

& in this Spoken
Law thank God

the message can get lost.
Back behind the book is a beforeness.
Before the thing written thickly in the book
is a breath breathing. Before the breath
is a breather. That means a pause
or silence or a rest. Or one who pauses
her mouth half-open at my ear
about to speak. Or not. Or let
the message loose into its breath.

The law
breathed its last
into a book.
Now it lasts
instead of breathing.

I want to get behind this book I find her breathing.

Early Spring Day Along the Housatonic

Water the quick anemone. We flower.
There was a sheer oil like rain
on the soft clean machinery.
It was the Derby Dam two months ago,
the river of such associations
lovely cold the timid bungalows
below the sluiceway, wide channel
for summer but there were no boats
though the last of March it had been 90.

Too many details. There's a library
where all this is stored. Woodstock
where it's cooler. The dam controls
were navy grey spelt gray. The road
ran by the river then crossed the dam
narrow, a diphthong. Thirty years ago
one would have thought of sabotage.
Now her feet are free of shoes,
zori on the car floor but her shapely
feet are naked on the controls.

Soon the houses would be opened up
smelling of winter and linoleum.
The old tv still seems to work
—only channels 3 and 8. The rain

presently is washing blue rooves—
gummy kind of shingle, tar-like,
gulls sit there often. Wood
has been so good to us all these
hundred hundred thousand years.

But in Woodstock even the old are young
and no one admits. *Ne passera*
they have been crying forty years.
Even the young are. The sad cocaine.
The library's books are old too,
expensive art books locked
away in a grilled-door manger.
I'm always 5 years old when I walk in
gulpy and foolish, awk and ward
since the alternative is to be
a ponderous half-celebrity, a poet

or other unreal river dammed
a few civil minutes so I dont drown
these competent handsome librarians.
I think about the rain in Derby
(here it is midnight, Hudson, dry)
and a daylight building in Woodstock
across the street from the laundromat.
If I try to read my eyes keep staring
out at the wash being tumbled forever

around and flop around and flop I'm down
at the bottom of the page without a clue.
I am as bad as a politician glad with names
or I am a pelican who eats all manner
fish. Mountain, river, dam,
the spindly, oily, navigable rain.

Dont you find it lonely with
all and only those memories? I do.
Consider the bungalow a-port
of the one futzing outboard moving

against the shore where taxes live.
There are people now say in New Haven
who'll come up open your door soon,
house. Ice-box will not smell bad.
There is a dead rat under the stove.
The mayonnaise jar full of plastic spoons
promises its own kind of welcome.
There is a piano. She sits down
horrified to be here again. Her father

is talking to the dog. Her hands reflect
hours applied to Mozart and Bach.
It makes the dog nervous mother thinks.
A walk is gone for, the piano
is returned to, supper is brought in—
a huge flat square cardboard box.
The love that bonds them here is real,
it is our only real religion
and sometimes I think it is our only love.
It trusts the orderly power of dams

up to and not including dreams.
When it is night the father sleeps
back at his desk at the Press,
sometimes his secretary undresses him
reverently caressing his socks.
He half-wakes and groans and turns.
The dreams of a mother are vivid and sad,
full of premiums unpaid, wallpaper

crawling to the floor. Never will she tell.

But the pianist who has been
dreaming all day is used up by midnight.
She curls in a ball. The dog.
The brother arrives from Cambridge
addled with dope, he sleeps
on the sunporch davenport, the dog
is continually disturbed. Night,
but I mention no names. Cartoon
of lovers, families, houses. Why
not believe the dream is solid and holds?

Because the spillway runs all day
all right. Some fine day will break:
anyone can tell that just by looking.
At anything. Rain so soft
the windows seem surprised, undone.
A bowl of eggs on the oilcloth'd table,
organic, bought from the farmer.
At some point in the night everyone
worries about the boat. Mother

hopes soon to eat a lobster.
Brother is learning Chinese.
Some nights she prays the dog will die,
her father is so lonesome with it.
He is lost out there now, his boss's hand
easy on the back of his neck, feel
of a warm dishcloth loving him. He whimpers.
She hates the piano. She hopes he
will stop using that stuff, those things.
He hopes the weekend passes fast.

It is not that men are frightened of the rain.
The bridge it first looks like is stalwart,
everything can cross. It is not that thinking
is difficult; it is so sensual to think
that most people are afraid of it.
You cant think without skin, lung, heart—
that is the mystery. I doubt very much
there's a book in the library that doesnt say so.
It is not that mystery itself is terrible

but men who have mysteries to disclose
are pompous and awful. Dont believe them
except when they talk about machinery
or sometimes the rain, or times when they remember
who played left field for the Boston Braves
or what happened to whom when the river rose
before the dam was ever built and houses,
cars and cows swept down into the Sound
with empty mayo jars bobbing in the surf.
Last year's flies likewise come back to life.

But in Woodstock what would I gather?
A hook for her hair. A book
to lie on her other side at night
to shape the imaginative breeze.
Some nutritious tao fu not to overdo.
Turkish apricots. Pistachios.
Technical reports on dbx's.
Details "without significance"
the pastor said, "beatnik bluff,

hedonistic precisions, soft junk."
I could almost believe he had suddenly
seen through the rain. Some orange honey.

Across the street the Christian Science church
surrounds itself with little woods
right there on the main drag, "no priest
but the perfected man." The rain
over Connecticut was true, blue
grey dam wheels and gears, tubs and ladders,
could have been anywhere at all

where the beautiful intelligence of men
commands a river. A book. A bungalow.
Old Scott's catalogue, stamps of Ingermanland,
Obock, Montenegro. Magazines
to read while you wait for the Book to open,
the sun stream down Tinker Street and hard
driving rain beat past in, the devil
abusing his wife, the wind up on Mead's
Mountain disguised as an Indian:

"I owned all this junk once, even the blue
grey paint on the battleships. I kissed
it goodbye as the expression goes.
I like to hear her play *Carnaval*,
fat march at the end of it. Beauty
is the one thing that is not opinion.
For its sake I let everything go. It fell
32 feet per second per second down past Canopus
where the imaginal world of my motherfather
hums in the dreams of rainsoaked pilgrims."

It is formal, it is perfectly willing
to end the way ordinary things do.
The librarian holds a book on her lap.
The brother wakes up before anybody.
"From the Housatonic to the Hudson once

all one nation," he remembers
and stares at the uncooperative river, clear
boundary of nothing at all. The gulls
are pawky. But the boats are awake.

Gacela

Are there at evening shuddering palaces
Where among shadows the moths go broke for light

Is there a broken shutter banging in the wind
Or is she just a breeze in a book?

But nice feral muscles of the sumac night play
Let lovers whisper among the transistors—

Under noise a continent of calm goes on
Right at the core of the clatter of hardware.

We are tender in the treasuries of tomorrow,
Our hands caressing switches that speak the light.

The Shortstop

Pick up the ball and hold it
while you analyze the vectors
of the heart. To describe
for one last time this town
knowing where every street goes
and who lives there. And why.
Where does the money come from?
The old house on the corner
has been painted brown.
Your dog never came home.
To analyze the spaces
inside a broken house. To touch
her again where she's truest,
most impossible to describe.
To find all the mythologies
her name opens up, to enter
that museum or laboratory
or bedroom or terrible porch
on a summer sunset there is
no one at all in the street.
Then throw the batter out.

The Dismembered

The sex they do against me in the streets leaves me poor as a star in the attics of a painful century. "Better century," I hear you say, but you forget anaesthesia. You forget radio—which is good, it frees, it frees most people from that burden of incessant telepathy which is mine. My burden is your mind, dont you know that? Sometimes I'm glad to bear.

How they choose anyone but me makes them eccentric, me mad, mad to care, crazy, cold as a fish, full of monsters I am slated to become. I burn with desire, and have since my seventh year, I am a prodigy of claim upon, upon all your beauty. You who go to sleep and smile, can you imagine the need that never sleeps, that slakes itself with excess and austerity and denial all, no difference, the orgy or the cellula alone, can you, what it means, when, the mind itself is burning?

These poets who translate horror from language to language! Safe in the non-committal zoo of surrealism, what do they know of the dark? The dark is not some logical proposition to be couched in these terms or those. The dark is the absence of propositions. The dark is not an image, convenient, a commodity that like a quarter adds up in some pig bank.

It is a crucifixion where you are the Christ and you dont believe in Christ but why are you hurting? The dark is not something to sell, to translate from French into what you think is American but is the foul syntax of inattention. The dark is not Spanish, not a lemon at midnight or to sit on a wall still warm from the sun. There never was any sun but me in this universe. These vile poets who think the dark is something to say! It is a muscle that squeezes us out and sometimes we cry and sometimes the cry's a word. And sometimes not.

from Sentence: Section 3

grass blades spring back up beyond the treading foot
caress of arcane hips slow summer me
arousal of what stars left as if a town
mansioned intelligence resilience of the mind

still alive after four hundred years of equations
it shapes itself well grape arbor with green hose
chromatic accidents he thought of simple light
how wrong or here descending early church a barn

manger light where weed better friend than a flower
till some door closed anew her face revising
that was less than you dream all people
you have gazed into a funny midbrain feeling

can touch an organ keyboard the spell of all
frequently disclaimed some claimed episodes of passion
as if he still could feel before him certainly
a certain flesh the reddening sumac saner than

to isolate as if the woman were the situation
not just a sensate item of to love to quiz
endless catechism of redemptive lust discourse
guesswork warehouse of the middle mind turned class

one thing after another until none until
a door dissembles sky he opens to rove more
no more and his pleasure is to stay just then
when the isolation carries him and his chaste

dreams are crowded in a dozened room
all that is singular in him requantified
there was a martyrdom of sense I argue
steepleless archaic church in principle I doubt

but still does what it does the grass the grazier
transparent history laundry on the line
darkened kitchen mortified by morning
to see the swell confusion of our purposes

all the books he never read repeat in him now
revenge to make him write them who speaks
his way into a door opens on a hallway of diminished fact
to touch her story and confound it with his path

forgive him into silence as a dog falls quiet
as so many piemen hurry to dumb fair
life of the trees unhinging tickle my ankle
unfurled gonfalon of fleshy sense this mute sorority

I adore thee who in singularity escaped to sign us
great glad exposition of the bang we still are
tacit diagram of every music every sentence
speaks a detail of thine everlasting physics

pebbles from the beach also brought home
to say an ocean sense but still be meek
and not to endorse the rhetoric of credences
to overwhelm the simple song of sense

who heard has been always hearing
I am the curtains in you opera I am your hand
green hose curled in grape arbor oak over Methodism
time our mind my awesome principal released

a suavity of conflicting purposes only apparently
to believe everything do everything until the lust
opens and becomes a body shaped like her but made
of justice and augmenting light specific arguments

responsible design innovation inner city
remorse redeem unspecifying syntax of
anarchic hedonists at last true citizens
to best become you and the worst go out

there is a sunlight on this news today
a fresh tire a pair of socks a dictionary sought
a blade of this leaf analysis crushed to savor
the otherwise pure water of our satisfaction

not what is it words do or how they mean
but how can I turn from what they're always saying
force them to serve me who always serve themselves
that abstruse questioner whose dreams our language is

how can they always be meaning in
from a place before meaning and keep telling
what we dont mean and will not do and still
it bears in upon us and no way to stop them

where even the fashions of language disclose
a mode of infinite analysis infinitely ready
to do the will of what will it is that savvies
the system we speak before we know its sense

"cathected" she said and my heart catches the tune
riven philosophies of world disorder here succumb
to all the dreamt doors I couldnt lock last night
the wolf at one bare arbor girl at a third

a man said the name of a base disease bare arbor
beerbottle lost in grass I sleep at the center
infinite web that brings to me here
the trembling info of your furthest message

this camarilla of discourse that never stops
mercying its motives to the city to the world
my peace I give of this immortal day
this conspiracy of light to know my mind

language is a circle whose circumference
is nowhere and whose center's everyone
language whose circumference is someone else
whose center self is vine freighted with wine

wine fruited with destinies the esters
of our long hope Europe immaculate America
never the names of things alone this paraclete
who comes to you when I am gone the valley

a sail cathected with her meaning
hurries the harbor White Sea steeples mute
philosophy to protect my sacred doubt
till the door wakes up from its dream of passage

Evening

A ladder going up into the tree
it is France maybe
a person comes to pollard his pears
or train them espalier
to face the setting sun and now
sits in his house drinking cool water when
some boys come mischievous to delete
his step-up highway.
The tree is empty. The ladder
is shoved in a culvert.
God is alone with the pears.

Cathedral of the Incarnation

Standing below the huge wooden crucifix,
looking up, acute angle,
close, looking up
as I have always looked up
in doubt or love distressed
to see
that man, a thin man,
not like me,
lifted up maybe but looks dragged down by gravity
drawing me up also, how,

that this is what the incarnation means,
or brings, this sleepy agony
it looks
above the world

what it means
when everybody in her difference
does it right,
everybody's right and this becomes.

And then it was night
and Nicodemus his dark disciple
came with a hundredweight of myrrh and aloes
to embed him

in the garden in the garden
mulched in these mortal aromatics down
against an eternity
that comes tomorrow

that came

and amid this bleak excellence of churchly, this
pocket cathedral up from the Salisbury Plain
all the stones
of resurrection

a gamble that this so thin a man
takes with closed eyes

before he simply dies.

Gethsemani

Kneeling there on the ground in the garden all through the night, he whispered quickly but distinctly the name of every person who ever lived upon the earth or ever would live here. He asked if anyone would help, or take his place. We all said No.

The Tower of Babel

Certain men decided to build a tower that would reach heaven. Week after week they toiled on the plain where bedrock, the planet's primary shield, offered surest foundation. The tower rose ever higher and the works ran smoothly. One day heaven looked down and saw the building coming close to it. Heaven grew confused and disorganized. The former unity of its purpose and consistency dissolved.

Heaven fell. Great flecks and patches of heaven dropped, landing on the tower or its builders. "We have reached heaven!" some cried. "Heaven is all over my hands!" one of them noticed.

There seemed to be no further point in completing the tower. Or, more precisely, it was not generally realized that the tower had never been finished; even the canniest builders tended to confuse the structure itself with the conscious goals they happened to have in mind. So as far as we can tell, the tower still stands unfinished, and no one can say where it actually could go.

Spring Sonnet

Love, do not be more clever than the heart.
Do not be clearer. Ever be more, love,
but do not be clearer than the heart.

Do not be clear do not be clever, love,
be more than clever love, be the heart.
Do not be than. Be not clear, be love.

Be more than be. More than the heart, be clear,
more heart than clear, more love than heart, be more
than be more. Do not clear the heart ever,
do not be clever, be love ever more.

The clever do not love, do not ever love.
The clever do not clear the heart, the heart
clearer than not be. The clear do love.
More than love be clear not ever. Be heart.

Elements of Moral Semiotics

1.

Can I mark the paper in the red of heart's love
art's blood herself exposed
granting to the senses what is mind's?

2.

Can the repetition of a complex carpet
lead the way to and through original
eastern cities of its enterprise to all such design?

3.

Can design foregrounded in the sign
liberate the carnal mind from such affections
as liberate themselves the mindly hand?

4.

Can I touch you in such way and only such
that the womanly prehension of my hand
incorporates the manly theory of our wills?

5.

Can I speculate while making love
the assembly of interactive powers
who bask above us light in our dark mass?

6.

Can I in connection so secure my thought
that the rainbow turns inside out inside
the closet where I guard my science—

7.

so that learning lore and love at once pour out
in the conniving of a midday coming
not otherwise exalted than a number is?

8.

Can I write the number down then
that by its Quality represents
the art of what its Quantity presents?

9.

Can I know a circumstantial air
such that heart sign and number say
isomorphic urgencies you understand?

∞

Seek out the far capillaries
for instance in the fingers where

through skin you flush with color
you can touch the other universe

that reaches out its hand
to sample yours. Think

how the blood cell in its passage thinks
past and future what for me is present,

faintly conscious of its journey
down my arm. All its times are now.

So I sit in a white room at noon
knowing that no one can escape us.

It is a matter of defining love
so that time itself takes cognizance

and sings through weariness and loss
How can you grieve? She is somewhere.

My boyhood was a raft of poems
but the marsh was real, a light
I later claimed as William Mount's light,
smooth-faced miscegeny of flesh and water

and where Whitman saw the actual bird
and lifted it, a general of the Vast Imaged Nation,
I saw only angels. And from their turbulence
in water at the sedge roots I took
for my garment the burlap web of the particular,

ever after trying to find, and finding, that angel light
in this and that.

        My Paumanok
was an infinite book, but intricate and mine,
blurred adventures of all the old heroes
to become I simply am.
                Wherever I may have come from
it is enough now that down in the bay
a yacht leans forward in high wind,
spinnaker cheeked out, white-flanked, the whole
of her quivering.

∾

When the brokers were raining on Wall Street
their soft knobby bodies hitting the pavement like news
I too was travelling towards the earth.

Slower, looking around, I saw explorers
decipher Mongolia, watched the men who would be my uncles
swill fat new beer in public, watched Nazi lunatics,
saw Ethiopians dying, Yeats addressing the senate,
Artaud running around Paris in magical circles, a small
man in the Australian desert was singing to me.

I couldnt make out the song, he moved bones on the sand
I couldnt understand. James Joyce read to Lucia—
I hurried to this condition where such sense could be made
and saw him sip green wine at evening. But a small
man in Australia was singing to me. I tried

to understand, I could only read his hands, I took hands
for my own, I took voices, I moved one last time like a lord
finding my mother's face. I listened,
I took bone, I let myself down in summer rain over Brooklyn
into the empty continent between the two musics I heard.

Nothing was speaking but the bones of her face.

The Nature of Metaphor

A man rises from the toilet in a public bathroom. He flushes, and begins to do up his trousers. His waistband is closed but his fly still open when the toilet begins to overflow violently. Horrified by the sudden upwelling of the primordial and irresistible flood, he rushes out of the bathroom to the corridor. A woman is standing there. She sees this man with gaping fly apparently hurrying towards her. Horrified by this primitive and menacing energy, she runs out of the building gasping. Outside, a man sees a woman escaping in obvious terror. Disheartened by the primal fear of a frightened woman, he runs away, away from her and from whatever she is escaping. As he runs, a girl on the sidewalk looks back over her shoulder and sees this agitated man rushing at her. Horrified by the primal threat of rape and aggression, she runs down a side street. Several women are walking in her direction, but perceiving her evident alarm, they wheel about and flee before her. A child playing at the curb sees the women running towards him. Horrified by this primal incursion from the realm of mothers, the child runs for his life. He runs until he can run no more, then sinks down sobbing under a bush, among the green myrtle in the north corner of the little park in our neighborhood.

from Postcards from the Underworld

I.

In that country there is a heap of millet
by the side of a road you have to pass

the rain does not wet it and each
passerby must nick one
and only one seed from the pile
and swallow it unchewed
disturbing as few as he can of the other grains

some of which will inevitably fall
and those that fall
slide into the human world and are born as human souls
with all the business of finding bodies
ahead of them

and he whose finger dislodged them from the heap
has them on his conscience until they in turn
pass by the mound of millet and make their choice

Far up the road the original eater
feels an unaccountable relief
a wind springs up and parts
what he thought all along was the blue sky

and whips its veils open

and he hurries into the next country
feeling the soft spring wind on his soft throat.

8.

In that country there is a kind of butter
that makes you think it's later than it is.
They spread it not only on the crusty bread
but on the road too and the rocks
and when the pilgrim slips and slithers his way there
finally it is still only morning

no matter what he thinks.
Everywhere there are stairs going down
when he slides down them
there is a country where there's another kind of butter
and lots more stairs
all going down.
There is never an end of going down.
After a long time the pilgrim eats some butter
tasting his fingertip behind the grease.

10.

In that country there is a woman
who leans against a door
the pilgrims come and watch her body
from various angles
watch it make contact with the wood

or stand away
watch the contours of the light
let between her body and the wood

and by these signs if they are signs
they interpret where the door goes
and when it will open to let them in

some of them wearied of this investigation
or their own interpretations
sit on the grass and watch the woman
hoping her face will teach them
by a sign even they cant mistake

they sit around the doorway and braid flowers
if there are flowers at their season
or else study the lady and her interpreters

as from time to time some pilgrim
looking no way different from the others
stands up or walks up
politely elbows past the woman and goes in.

II.

In that country there is a pool
where travelers fresh from dying wash their wounds

they bathe and feel renewed
and go on with their excursion
their skin healthy and intact

but the pool if you look down there

through the lucid quiet water
is full of wounds
bloody intricate and rich along the bottom
like the map of any human country.

12.

In that country there is a telephone
from time to time atop a wooden fence
or hung on the side of a willow tree

its purpose is uncertain
but travelers weary or benighted
sometimes pick it up and listen

they feel the familiar contours in their hand
so like a fruit you cant eat
but the phone feels strange to them here

and the feeling in their hand is stronger
than anything the phone tells them
though they listen to the comforting dial tone

and sometimes punch the buttons
and even wait for the ring to be answered
by one of those voices who answer

who speak the same maddening language
which is all you ever hear down here
you cant make out a word of it

though it all sounds just like english
spoken quickly and sincerely
in a room a little bit too far down the hall.

17.

In that country there is a hoof
that comes down from the sky once in a while
and just stands there
a hoof and a slender furry shank
going up as far as they can see

they come and stand around the hoof and argue
this is Pan's foot
or this is the hoof of her cow or this
is herself's own footstep

and when the hoof is gone
disappearing sometimes in the middle of their talk
it leaves a crater filled with milk

each drinks from it or abstains
in accordance with his nature and beliefs
about the nature of the hoof

the milk tastes like any milk
somewhat sweet and flat and when
night comes it shows the moon clearly
bobbing on the pearly surface like a nervous mouth

24.

In that country they have a distance
that fits between two people like bread in a toaster.
They still can see each other, still can talk.
But the distance is there. They feel
like different cities in the same country

244   *from* UNDER WORDS (1983)

or different countries in the same world.
One wakes up and finds the other gone:
But the distance is still there. He carries it
the way a blind man carries his hands.

The Head of Orpheus

When Orpheus walked beneath the trees
all the leaves were Eurydices

when Orpheus looked into a well
he saw the skies of hell

when Orpheus took up his lyre
he saw his funeral pyre

on which the Maenads tossed
his scattered limbs and hissed

"Everything he did was wrong:
love and theory, wife and song"

yet when they picked up his head
they kissed his mouth and said

"All the lies these lips told
kept us from ever growing old—

now keep them wet eternally."
And Orpheus saw them throw it in the sea.

Ode to Language

To put on shoes and be sophisticated
—it really was a creamy trumpet
Miles Davis made—or gleam waxy
and smile along the El-shadowed street
through all the synaesthesias of weary language
patient, at our command, like an old dog.

Faithful animal! Endure
Tehran, Stella by Starlight, Nautilus
machines, the skanky fantasies
of men no longer young, the rough
edge of graffiti, borrowed vices
of exurban novelists, the price of glass.

Break me. Come to me
with burrs in your fur, tell me
where everything has ever been.
Growl at me if I sleep, wake me
with your dependable craziness.
Birds plummet and you fetch them
wet from your mouth. Women weep
in San Francisco. Only you

are ever different.

Variations on a Poem of Stefan George

Windows where I once with you
At evening looked into landscape
Are bright now with a foreign light.

Path still runs from the door where you
Stood without looking around
Then curved down into the valley

At the turn once more you lifted
To the moon your pale face.
But it was too late to call

Darkness—silence—stiff air
Sinks as it did then round the house.
Every joy you took away.

I.

Windows where I in selfish air
looked stiff into evening
wanting you to stay

But I was the path, the dark
valley that sucked you away

was my strange light, my call.

Everything you took with.
What is left is a joy
like a pale face in moonlight

not sure which way it looks
as the door falls down the valley,
as the door becomes landscape

and you come back constantly
along the selfish path I am
waiting at evening for your call.

2.

You went and I window.
I am selfish with light
and I am stiff with calling.

I am the path where you
once turn round too late for silence
too late for moons

I am stiff as glass because the light
shows you only going out and coming back.
Come back the way a face

sinks around the house and makes it stay,
the way a moon turns
into a window and the landscape

runs from the door.

3.

At evening you look in.
I am stiff with calling
and you are bright with doors.

It was too late to look around,
the joys of valleys are a silence
you took with. The turn

was where the evening door
fills with foreign joys and we stand.
We stood. Once
with you at
foreign landscape
to the moon
too late for
you curved
down into silence

4.

windows where I once with door
summoned a turn in the path
and the moon looked over her shoulder

till the landscape filled with standing still
come back the way a place
becomes foreign and a door looks around

and you bend around the silence
and your face lifts in the stiff air
and veer back what once curved away.

5.

Stiff in your valley
your face sinks round me
and I am bright with a strange window

6.

in the land a shape I saw
since noon, too late to call
I stood in hell with framed unlight—

woe to standers! oh to have your name
to shower down in, starry light!
fate knocks loud from the door,

time bleaches anger,
a tomb to roof my spite—
jungle of glass from which we looked

I am made simple by distance.

7.

and this land shape I saw
has you in it turning back
and lifting to the moon again

the foreign windows of your face
so they will shine for us,
those stars whose unlight

frames hell as a house
from which you curved away—
but now the bright silence

veers you home.

8.

I am my body and I want you back
I am my body and I am my mind I
am my body and I want your mind

whatever I am I want your body
curving back to look at me
the way a face looks at the moon

and I want your moon to be my mind
and your mind to be my face and I want
to look around me and find you

I want to look up at your face
the way a window hears a house
and a door falls through landscape

endlessly opening. Then the dark
turns silent and only your name
stands in the mind of the door.

9.

You turn back and see the star
that brightens with your tears

It is a name to hold in mind.

A valley to revisit.
The mail never comes, you have
to bring it to the door.

It is always noon in this jungle—
in the darkness a silence sways,
tries, tears the emulsion of an image.

We are together—then
bleach the dark and turn
lifting again your pale face

to my body. I am your door
you are my path we are our house—
light finds your name

to shower down in once for all.

10.

Moaned, and I mean you more
the want I do you turns me
to the door, to spite all calls
and still call out. To veer
towards you and leave every valley

and find you where a star *stands*.
Stall me under hedges, bright
with seeing you again I turn the path
itself into a house, the land

into a window, time to a door
and we stand together not looking back.

11.

Find a star where it shines with tears
evenings in the land, shape you saw
since noon: hell with framed unlight.

Fate knocks loud from the door: woe to
standers. Oh name to shower
down in! Stall me under box hedges,

by your care warmed, no male ever
moaned. Time bleaches angers.
Thought is where to spite tomb-roofs—

jungle—swaying—starry light
sings between emulsions. A house.
All is freed, and names you mine.

12.

Fenster wo ich einst mit dir
Abends in die landschaft sah
Sind nun hell mit fremdem licht.

Pfad noch läuft vom tor wo du
Standest ohne umzuschaun
Dann ins tal hinunterbogst.

Bei der kehr warf nochmals auf

Mond dein bleiches angesicht.
Doch es war zu spät zum ruf.

Dunkel—schweigen—starre luft
Sinkt wie damals um das haus.
Alle freude nahmst du mit.

∾

I want to tell you
something simple
how when we sleep
together our breath
goes somewhere
I dont know I guess this
where it must

and seems there
an ordinary air
flowers could breathe
from our two mouths
so close together
a single complex idea
they proliferate
petal by petal
until it has a single
name, like "rose" or
today the "daffodil" is
ready
    yellow
        only
the name is simple
after all
and I've told you

one more lie

tell it with me
until we can think
of something longer
than flowers
something purple
something instead

—the earth is tired
of comparisons

Doors

Suppose you didnt know what a door is. That it opens, for instance. It would seem a different part of the wall, thinner, more resonant. A decorative rectangle set in the wall, an embodiment of some geometrical mystery like the Golden Section. It would seem tantalizing to someone trapped in the room—a perverse, mean tease: the wall is thin here, soft, but still unpassable. How little it would take to get through the wall, yet you cant.

Suppose you didnt know what a door is, that it can open, that its resistance defines the zone of least resistance, but that zone requires a deft use of something learned, a knack, a skill: twisting the knob and pulling. Or pushing. Even if you got as far as turning and pulling, if the door were the kind that opened outward, you'd still never guess, never get through.

Suppose all round us there are things like doors in things like walls and we never knew.

from A Stone Wall in Providence

I.

At dawn the sun investigates the blue copper dome
of the Christian Science church and at nightfall

the same formal acorn inhibits the roseate light.
Then it is dark. It is winter. The long propositions

of romance, as much a part of us as cracks in glaze
are part of porcelain, become hard to see in this light.

Hard to hear. The heart is always an investigation.
Let me draw inferences from difficulty. What is hard

is always beginning and comes to an end no more
than the pattern on the scarlet Bokhara carpet does

though it meets an ornamental border and resumes
all the alternative directions its mystery is heir to

thing after thing, a hope of its own,

grace of its own. Isolate in openness, in the hope of change,
old me in a new city, selfish as colors.

3.

About that power: it is the serum of questioning
that flows through the blood of the mind. The mind is current

through all flesh, it is a river, it is this river,
slaty pewter, sluggish under the arches at Fox Point

slowly getting around to be sea. The mind is its occasions,
faithful to the cloth and to the swell of hip

that minds the cloth. It is not nowhere. Cleverness of water
to pry everywhere is also its cunning. It can freeze a season

but there is always spring. The dome comes back at morning
far beyond the huge playing field where the girls at hockey

trot with cold red knees under plaid skirts with civil squeals.
And the mind has something to work with again, weary

of the ulcerating languages of night it gnaws at, strange grammar
whereby three a.m. turns into sleep and sleep into dawn

like one long sentence in whateverese.

9.

It is a desperate act to be among my kind, cafe.
Two back to back working, a third squeezes between—women,
    wisdoms.

For wisdom is by no means single. There is no ultimate
    agreement

except to keep talking. Keep the fasts of time, the purple ferias
    that make me strange

wondering who died in the night. Who came to life?
What moves the light to break like news

upon us in the shapes of them hurrying through a pattern
that can be decoded, long after, memory tracking the bee paths

how the three women move behind the counter, leaving traces
    that recur,
themselves as formal interruptions of this formless thinking.

Or behind veiled windows still translucent families move
through the warfare of their interactive distances, psyched-out
    gazeteer

of chance apartments channeling their anger and granting such
    peace
as space has in its mercy to bestow: bringing close, leaving far, a
    soft corner

to feel sorry for myself in, sick, or lick the wounds. And in the
    mean
called time among all this yummy flurry I like so well, the wall
    stands.

10.

Its evident stillness we are told is pure deception, a covenant of
    molecules
to align in such a way that we are tricked by a shimmer of
    solidity

and hence keep off the grass. Do not see (except from here, high
  window)
the centerfielder suddenly appear to catch a fly then vanish back
  of trees

from which their languid cries lit softly (storm windows already
  down)
to curse the undercurrent silence. That was Pindar's golden harp,

a shout of the exerted body suddenly plucked from the silent
  bowl of sky,
a noise out of which narrative uncoils. Decode this music. Say
  what the shout

means to say, your father's black-sailed ship, your romance with
that sly Cappadocian hero. How your mother watched a snake
  unfold

down near the waterfall and from its springtime stretch decided
she would make you with your father's instrument. Every noise
  notates.

What we hear is seldom what is there. It is an index of some
  history
we strive to know, and by knowing unite it with our own future
  till

time and memory are one thick strand united, stubborn as a wall,
and just this endless self-referring rope or running it is my will to
  break.

II.

We come back at last to the simplest knowing:
a window pretending to be a self in a world of selves.

The things that hurt us are easy to remember,
a foot, a tooth, a number. A dentist in Paris

who did not listen to your pain. A need. I have lain
beside you and not known. We have not known

and all the same the field across Arlington
fills up with light, a marching band, a forest of rooftops

to say some last farewell to an immense city
we will go on living in, live forever, in, though

at this moment and in this eye it goes from us
passing in slate grey and umber and blue.

Shade comes through the window too, for all the hot porches,
yellow walls, graduate students at deft affairs next door.

Do not forget me, treetop, though you fall your leaves
and drown the book of my attention beneath the waves of light.

20.

So under the anemones a woman is studying her book.
Under its roof a house sits dreaming of slate. The rock dreams
    moss.

Now I know you, wall. You are the sentence spoken in
    childhood,

ground onto the blackboard with wartime chalk, the verdict,

sentence of forgotten words but whose shape teaches every
          proposition.
What better sense could I make? Proportion. Architrave, dusty

giant bodies of the gods. Or is all the body dusty, chalk dusty,
and all the books, their gutters full of the dust we use to think?

When a god knows his death is near, dust falls on his brocade.
His armpits give off suddenly the smell

of all the sweat the workman he never was poured out
in honest but unmindful labor. His guitar strings come untuned.

And therefore I look at this squat dome and say again
how precious this sort of life is wherein it can be said:

A black boy runs and I am he. A dog runs with him and it is me.
I see him and am seen and am the seeing. In which the method
          comes:

To cherish every difference and know there is no difference.

Looking

Once when I read the funnies
I took my little magnifying glass
and looked too close.

Forms became colors and colors
were just arrays of dots
and between the dots I saw the rough bleak
storyless legend of the pulp paper
empty as the winter moon

and I dreaded it.
I had looked right through,
when I wanted a universe
that sustains
looker and looking and the seen
forever, detail after detail
never ending. And all I had found
was between. But between
had its own song:
Find it in the space between—

it is just as empty as it seems
but this blankness is your mother.

from Those Who Are Beautiful/A Sonata

Rest a hair of color on a lot of air
Seed marigolds and wait for white
An obvious imposition on the mind
Keep me in your heart
To be this agriculture too
So many chitterlings in this cauldron
And my burnt thumb tastes you
Serene hysteric with large eyes
Immensely wise and hardly knowing
Now is the time
Before you get older or I get young
The way time's hydraulic flushes
Certainly leave large spaces
Or where would the music go
Lady blow me blue
The nature of what is personal imitates music
Fond father uncle of nine a desert
Advertises for its ruling rock
Come do my job I need some help
Sit up late taking me seriously
Every lover says obsess obsess
So I'll be no lover longer
And this quick kiss won't tie your hands

Any living room looks better for fish

266   *from* UNDER WORDS (1983)

There are slow release feeders for fish
We can leave the tank alone for days and not hurt fish
I swear Ladie my tongue is one of such
Fish and feeder both you'll find
Lambent in your fish bowl I your mica castle
And all I am is good for you again
Your house and never be possessed
Your hands and never be obsessed
Your nose and never be plain
Your hair and never be rage
Your arm and never be curt
Your belly and never be mute
Your knee and never be local
Your fingertip and never sand
Your two ears and never Solomon
Your important neck and never Tahiti
Do not hide your heart your navel and your left hip
Do not have a shy shank
Do not let your elbow learn Norwegian
Do not be wise o do not be wise
There are birds here that could make two of us
Dinner for a star and cheese for a child
Your eyelid and never a Ferrari
Your eyelash and never a boat
Your nostril and never philosophy

Your chin and not a postage stamp
Your tonguetip and never night
Shimmer o do not be wise
Grow young without apologies
Your buttock and never a bible
Your shoulderblade and no sheep
Your nape and no oracle
Never be wise o never

O shimmer and not relax
Be wise neither nor soft
Your ankle and never the Bastille
Your sex and never a senate
Your breast and never a prayer

All we have are the names of things
Not so
All we have are names and scarcely things
Scarcely things are for the having
Names are for the calling
Calling is beautiful and what we have
Is busy with calling

The Rainmakers

The groups of God
broken into world,
morsels chosen
from that curious Hellenistic author
The Demiurge
whose multitudinous works
we daily anthologize,

persuaded by French masters
and local mistresses
to be wise,
                  to live in a world

(this one)
if only for the sake of the weather.

They run the weather,
the rainmakers
want us to like it,
sell us the sexy
isotherms of semiotics,
the structure of structure,
                  o Fashion
is a savage god.

2.

Poetry tries "to bring all its experience into natural grace"
says Duncan, and keeps the numbers
current,
        the swells of speech
whose ordered passion
compels the restless lust of mind
into the presiding metaphor of dance
which here knows itself
as particulate movements

studied in noticeful economy,
physicist at cloud chamber
charming the incidents
to hold some place in natural speech
(trying to be natural!)
as if it really were a world we speak.

3.

And the numbers are not governors,
the numbers are white, every one is one,

wings of a jungle bird
analyzed into color as
one thing listening always to another,

an old woman visiting her bees.

Dampier's Voyages

In buying horses pay no heed to the haunch
but the eyes only, the slight
enlargement of the spirit that means speed,
or mild abatement of the wit
that speaks docility. And if a man
seek both qualities in one mount
he will not find it in this country.

So counselled I took ship
and found the contradiction
everywhere I looked,
but there were islands I have not visited
where energy and peacefulness
may look from the same eyes
like a green table in a wild garden
beside a wooden chair
the color time painted it,

and on it one sitting
crosslegged at the knee in repose
reading this book of travels
more with the mind than with the eyes
and those same eyes
lift from time to time
away from table and book

to the rim of the garden wall
barely to be seen beneath wisteria,
looking at the sun through shadows

and the legs recross another way
and the islands in the book
teem with wild swine crashing through
plantain and bananas, their hoofs
under wild spice trees
up to the hock in years and years of fallen cloves.

The Man Who Loved White Chocolate

There is an egg in the middle of things
a blue racer a kind of whip
to top the spin with, thus reify
(thingle) it, there is a mallet
tunking metal there is a frog
lucid gel that harbors comingstance
the drift of spawn along along,
there is a gong goes in the egg
wakes him from his appetites.

Be scant, new citizen.
Intellectual hedonism of easy things
well-made plays, craft
for the comfort of some buyer—
yet no shoe without its nail
—sails look cuter with no boats—
so many ways to get married

and live in affluence as you'd live in Spain
silently well-servanted on gaunt plateaux
surveying our meaty ruin: O vultures
(but they respond not, being robins,
sparrows, such, and common crows)
having their own jive no need of his

there is a white taste in his mouth
long row of stalwart fencing
dangled in his neighbor's light
unstrung from rollers and stretched
along the bordermind, a tooth
for you, muchacha, and (lachaim!)
a prick or two—galvanized roses—
in your hand. Willingly obey the dog.
Go. (He reflecteth darkness as
rehearsal for that sweet despair
that long Without)   blue flowers

red birds new grass a yellow chair
a flag of surrender run up
in the smooth colorless air. Eat me
said the day, I have never snowed,
never forgotten. Bird thuggee,
rattle-pinioned raptors throng
devour such offerings, raw
conversations between parted lovers
estrange him from himself. Some stars.
Admit that appetite is mostly mind
you're left only a little tool to lie with
—the cardinal almost orange in harsh sun
swelling towards the river where she sits
red vestmented chatting with a friend
who cut her hair too short—
who pulls me down? See, see
where an old chunk of weathery wood
checks, splits, gapes to show
Christ's lordly tulku in the firmament.
Even this, heart, is one more thing.

The talk is chaff from off some core,

coronal of disasters whose livid petals
one by one we dare to pluck. Blue flower
never found unless in losing.
Many a burnt hand, mortgaged mind,
undersapped foundation, leprous wall.
Leviticate, lixiviate, then levigate
—one more lie from the makers of the Pantheon—
in the harlot's church a dead emperor waits.
Le tombeau de your last concrete example.
Broad skated, high on the wave, prorsum, prow.

Hone your keel for such thick seas.
A moment after. How is she now,
and will her new car mend the distance?
Spill a road on whom go quiet
gyved by circumstance, not wearing a hat,
wind-tousled, a shy conquistador?
Malinche, remember she. So dark.
Weinend, klagend, Easter never,
hope not, live long, squill-blue, hurry.
The spring is in today, no wonder
like this wonder. A lamb in trouble.

Fondle you. What world does she generate
sexier than herself, and if none, bother,
she-failure, one more just plucked rose.
O she doesnt make things up,
the villainess, does she suppose
flesh's enough for flesh and talk for talk,
aye-bartering, yatter and sex?
Tisnt. Rub two random words together
to get a richer universe than any this.

Micron by turkey feather turning

we doubt our same black bodies and white bodies
because the difference is only a car only
on roads capable to go that we have made
and there's no finding He didnt find before
—the man who ate rice pudding
without necessarily liking and certainly
not despising it—one turns
and it is here—lactoglycodynamo
a kilocalorie or so to wake
what part of us can sleep—
red baubles on a spruce tree, April tinsel—
o the horn signal of the house on fire
whence even skeptics flee—here comes
the hook and ladders!—spirit searchlights
spotting a hasty ruin—hurry—
promise the little children something red.

Promise levanters a sensuous occident
and they'll come home, every sentence
is the whole of what he ever knows,
but he has no home to take them in,
that's rich, that's lips. In palaver
linger, between a breath and a breath
glimpsing true orient—as when the words
you suddenly see her mouth making
are only to make you look at her speaking

—at and in—beyond and never come home
—that were promised-lander's promise,
pure going! Pierce going, pang getting,
all at once a devious love-feast (a door
for him suddenly open) listen (opera
that curious machine ('feel my heart
beating where your ear hurries')

lords and ladies coltsfoot the periwinkle
blues (husband of a breast) (cantilever)

the man who loved white chocolate
loved a rumor of the sea
that one of those milky camerlengas would
(hard to see through tressures, hers, as
today she of the sky said, *treasures of cloud*)
float him to a book or book to him
sage under carageen an old unlogic
unlocking—the greatest mystery is analysis—
to demystify the very sense he sees them by,
utter,most,wise,ness, the continent.
Not by any mirror see your naked face.

White-stubbled cheeks a youngish mien
six finches at the window bumming seed
gloriosos full of chatter and
strumpet-minded he sees gold
beyond the greenwork of the day, spring,
lax, oil, tight in posture loose inside

I am the uncommitted
grotto of Natural Selection
what he thought when he went home
thinks him forever after or not ever
—the bust of Beethoven on the shelf
must mean something—take it
in small mouthfuls, mind—

look at the season you find a self in
so well calypso'd you'd
guess there is none, you'd be right,
stomachers on cold bacon, a chest

full of medals he cast for himself
George Sand's fingers trail along the keys
in private agonies of emulation—
I wear this hero's cross beset with jade
for the Campaign of the Hypothalamus,
this ruby wheel, this ivory spinnaker
for all my frowardness, mirror jabber,
this tuneful testament of thieves.

Towards the Day of Liberation

It doesnt matter what we see there

(the mouth is full of sense
no taste in listening
no sense to hear
what twists in the shallow water below the tongue)

(and if he says Listen! say
Drink the hearing with
your own ears, a word
is not to hear)

Language? To use language for the sake of communication is
like using a forest of ancient trees to make paper towels and
cardboard boxes from all those years the wind and crows
danced in the up of its slow.

A word is not to hear
and not to say—
what is a word?

The Catechism begins:
    Who made you?
    Language made me.
    Why did It make you?

It made me to confuse the branch with the wind.
Why that?
To hide the root.
Where is the root?
It lies beneath the tongue.
Speak it.
It lies beneath the speech.
Is it a word?
A word is the shadow of a body passing.
Whose body is that?
The shadow's own.

The Cloudherd's Song

Never having done anything ever but watch
and never having actually watched anything,

never having attended to anything but cloud
and never having touched one or learned

its numbers or colors or rightful names
(except once on the slopes above Darjeeling

I woke out into the morning and breathed you in,
mother of atmosphere, green air,

eternity, vagrant, the monsoon
had brought you and I took you entirely in)

I call you cloud and call myself yours.

Elegy

Alone alone is not a touch or need
to dwell with sheep archaic pastures
who was a rock small in sunshine builded
at last upon some pediment—prominent
carved with one more god's name.
Lust is terrible desert. The burnt lizard
and the parched lioness alone are able
to construe that name. Now the phone
sings and a thousand signatures
finally answer my mail. Cubist
conversations watch women pass
talking to one. So much skill
to be a martyr or fake an erection
because nothing is simply simple. *I will go*
because he borrowed my attention
but want to stay because I love your milk.
Transparent to show the works inside
fairy with dew or with the morn's pretenses,
streets, those false premises, leading
deeper into an unfathomable argument

I still have to pay taxes to.
City is all those women I do not know
to say the least or buses where I will not go,
bars choke on what I do not drink.

Still sitting on my lap so lift my hand
beneath your sweater that our eyes
bask in cognitive relations
before one more dawn comes back.
We are not a population,
we are one at a time ones,
not individuals but handily distinct.
"Mysterious, like everyone else."
Avid ascenders, satined in glory.
Our hearts are just like yours
you tell me—but not a city,
which is the sum alone of all our ignorance.
If it came down to it
would you have to sleep with me
to know what I mean or let me go?

Or would the last revision
leave a text as desolate
as the evening star just
before the full moon rises
in blue March—nothing
but words and what *they* mean?
Only a story storying no one,
chastely, ceremonious?
I want to come between you
and your lips, your graceful
concessions to this language
we drown in for our oxygen.

(Sleeping far away from one I love
is not so far, is not alone
the way alone is. It is a word
spoken and heard, the pause

before some answer comes.)
A slipper full of cream
to walk on stars with—
what a queendom you intuit
and frame it with your thighs
—pale borderers—play
chess for breakfast and
breathe all night long soft
wine of counterpanes and be
lush as any Apaloosa is for
meadows, any steel for
cantilevered bridges over
estuaries mobbed with birds,
pelicans, loons, shearwaters,
a man is an animal who looks
and lives in cities, steals
glory from the trembling dictionary—
while lust is a pigeon safe
on any roof, head of any
steeple open the church
and where are the here
in your hands I also come.

Gets me nowhere. It is sleeting outside
and wit is thronged with tasteless things,
combinations and resemblances, a feast
of cheap interpretations, a sleek
modern rhetoric in the slipslop rain.
Always hanging out in other languages,
or is it snow. Drove home slow
down the mountain and by the river
imaging certain blond adventures
I would not consent to if I could—

the heart has a chastity the mind might envy.
Give me a diamond to give it to you.
Make it hold water and break light
with blue promises. Flash after flash!
Desires are savages surrounding you,
respectful but determined,
chaste as knives,
these things that go on knowing me.
Fantasies protect you
from taking the real as real—
because they move, and that motion
is real although the mover's not
and he courses in an unearth landscape
chasing hot phantoms. But such
bright ghosts they are, with such soft hair.

Movement moves. Absolute predication
without an absolute to predicate.
Real worlds
have no rules,
just consequences.
No taste
without its mouth.

(if you talk long enough to the robin on the lawn
till your heartbeats and his hops are in sync
when he—ruddier at the breast, no bigger—finds
his worm, what do you find? A chill
of huntingness, a morning with no soap,
a sense that you are nobody, hence clean and true,
true as hot and cold, or things that come and go.)

The one you heard on the radio reading out loud

was a cloud. The wet slick on the porch roof later
was his idea. There's no harm in calling him a god
if you reflect that gods too have their limitations.
Cant have bacon for breakfast, for instance, or fast
like your girlfriend on green clay and psyllium seeds.
Or do anything about the world's misery they too
will ultimately share, even in Wagner, even
when their silk brocades smell funny and their pals
remember prior engagements and even the peaches
on the trees of heaven fall bitter pulpy on dead lawns.
Pray for the poor god who gives us comfort while he can,
wind and rain, a wise remark or two the thunder passes.

Examine the tracks of animals. Passing by night,
reading by the neat light of stars which way to turn
when there is no real way out. See how to run.
Under a pine tree the tracks gave out, a flurry
in the snow, then nothing. Where did it go,
such a big animal, a wounded deer, lost
by hunters who suffered their own distractions
and were not as intelligent as it was
to begin with? Where does an animal finally go?

The form released from killing and from craving.
The form released from fear. One daffodil
and then another, another, and she loves me.
To seasons we are like any beast obedient.
Indeterminate links to what determines us,
a boundary demarcation some fool pope proposed
—as between Spain and Portugal dividing
a thing called body from a world called soul.
And we are various, five heaps of praises, five
heaps of undetermined gypsy othering we call our own.
So many bodies it takes to be me, and what it is

is hardly anyone. There is no folly
like the myth of philosophy. From no landing strip
no airplane takes off for nowhere.

Jungle edges of an infinite population,
field effects of gossip. Local history.
Time was the man who. This was the idle boy
who grew to be the man who never rested.
I look back to long days of those summers
when I did nothing but dream and eat and read,
rose into reveried air, look back as
in the afterlife mind might look back
with chance compassionate nostalgia even fondly on
the soft awkward body that gave it so much trouble.

There is always a lonely house in the mind
where it is sad and black birds only
come to bring the news. Sometimes red
patches on their wings remind us Springtime
is still available She is really there The glass
fills up and empties The sky
is always empty. That is its gift to us,
its art, this emptiness,

to have a working knowledge of the world.
Little alabaster carved to seem a bird
with a whistle in its tail. South American.
It's hard to blow, soft breathy siffling.
The bird itself seems to have turned round
to see what our mad lips are doing now.
A bird like the Egyptian letter 'a,
glottal stop, orange beak, lazy eye,
posited on a rock of one substance
with itself, looking back, complete.

You can barely hear it in the next room
except you know that something odd is
happening. Someone is calling you.

from The Flowers of Unceasing Coincidence

173.

this quiver in the hand white belt white shoes
the man is old in summertime
and time true to its rep brought money
and he eats and on what bible is it sworn
that his dullness is not interesting it is
as any fish or box of books or some old war
only a bronze soldier remembers among the filthy fascinating
    pigeons

175.

pretend it is a ship
and what we feel
that's so like moving
is a meaning
and what pitches is uncertainty and
what rolls is the sumptuous
pleasure of having a body to be in
while the ocean itself
captains your brief ears
and guides you to blue places

177.

tooling this small thing
to meet its measure
square and cubic and by all

powers elated to the highest
energy by being just it is
a this a flower

207.

why did they teach us *anagke* the first day of Greek?
laddered wall spinnaker on a river signs
of that elopement by which we love
quickly outgrowing *Necessity* that junk food

222.

To be in not to be—
That is the answer.

228.

me too little flower
as of roadside chicory
dyed blue by the masters of resonance
to fit your hand or
what reaches out to me for
no other reason than I touch

235.

the names sleep on her skin
the names of fashionable things
beneath which her newness lay
ever touching never touched

236

a brick house my father thought meant no repairs
but then the mortar crumbles music comes
unstrings the courses and the naked sand
falls back to mere becoming—how can you stand up
house meaning what you thought her body meant

237.

for syntax frees
and meaning
is ownership
and this art
is for those with nothing to say
and trust only them
incandescent unowners of a transpiring text
This House of Prayer For All Peoples

300.

don't disconcerted by the drift of narrative
suppose coherence where's only the continuous

event seamless but story is one thread
chosen or self-chosen for a welt of misery

tiny island tiny house yard square yard high
much visited by geese who honk but do not sleep there

301.

it's who you sleep with after all that counts
after all the image form of substance
that spells your sleep and as you sleep
hungers beside you tangent snoring
each of you a boat the other floats in
dreamless through the endless dream

303.

Peremptory maiden whose blush Jersey meadows wear
perceptible from medium-size midtown buildings at Angelus
there's only one sun and only one moon and no one living
trusts them to live together ever. And so I name thee maiden
magdalene or hip of slim consenting hiddenness
for all your lush cosmetic *peau de lumière*
like me you hear moon's belly rumbling. And you fear.

372.

The Mekong like the Yangtze and the Brahmaputra
arises in Tibet but by its delta it has learned
the mortal sciences we teach so well down here
and like any local river has dead cows and broken barns

intricate raftwork of wreckage from our lives
like one of those soft novels nobody ever reads
you find covered with mildew in summer cottages
beside old Geographics with dingy photos of Tibet

508.

taking refuge
in the way things are
all the ornaments of emptiness
crest-jewel we wake up wearing
sun

509.

and I will be blacksmith of this light
and bent it with my fingers alone
nails of it into ankhs rainbows and omegas
until the earth is littered with horizons

512.

saying without thinking is so loveliest
like a blonde morning in Massachusetts
or October like an escritoire
stuffed with letters meant for you
and an opulent candle burning at high noon

513.

roofed with sky or lapis
there to be certain as a crossroads can
nothing somethingly forgot

squeeze the rock and leave the impress of your hand
there is a time in you when everything is soft
then count the birds to harden time again

515.

(*A small Noh play with the Ghost of a Fisherman*)

I killed to live
I thought
though I tried to give
little pain—taking many in my net at once
to give them the company of death
and now I prop myself
against this dying tree
and call to you
you in a language the fish taught me

524.

I feel most beautiful when I stare at the grain of wood
all those currents are running only here
and here is nowhere special, only here
and I stare till I forget I'm looking
a fence around a small field of
acts of knowing that cut the endless thread of talk
always on the side that falls, always in rain

525.

world balanced on the palm of my hand
Mount Meru by two fingers coaxed to stand!
And I call to my friend Friend!
I call to my mountain Mother teach me
how to open an open hand
and let what I have never touched fall from my grip

528.

I saw Orion
looking down on Los Angeles
warning me:
A love is one more day
trying to live by the rules of night.
And to these stars
a Khmer Rouge soldier also looked up
with tears in his eyes killing his friends
because of something he thought the light told him

627.

some say the Labyrinth was made
of one simple not very long word
on hearing which the monster, frightened,
fled to the center of himself
leaving only skin and horn and hair
to titillate the crowds of tourists come
to see the place where Ariadne lewdly danced

628.

err garden weather wander
the sweet tradition of being wrong

629.

run out of gas with you beside me
take the wrong turn up the mountain road
bring the wrong screwdriver for your machine
and pick a cave the sun shoots through at dawn
your rueful smile Jerusalem enough

632.

a citizen of nowhere
expecting nothing of the art
except the capacity to carve
verse out of distress out of
unsatisfiable appetite
and turn my own yammer
into a politics of light

In the Light

Where did I see you? In the mistaken light
between competence and performance

in the protestant light I cherish
dusty scarlet, light of a high church modest candle,
sanctuary light, real presence,

in the protestant light of presence,
in the presence of light, light
is always adequate

in the light between desire and performance,
in the mistaken light between
the rule and the sentence, the bleak
light over Kaminstein's Hardware,
lost marriages, all our olive natures
ancient, goat-gnawed,
in the dawning light between
desire and the expression of desire,

in the episcopal light
that makes you take off your violet shirt
and still your skin shows that color,
morning light coming in off the snow

in the snow light between danger and desire,
for lust driveth out terror
in the urbane light of South Kensington
between a museum and what it shows,
between a replica and an original, a door,
light of a door, light of your areoles
purple in the fluted light of my mouth
kissing them tight, in the light
that rides inside us on our tongues our hands
in the interpenetrant light between
Shakertown and Harrodsburg, in mountain light,
in the light inside a glass of wine,
a wine I never drink, light of absence,
where is your mouth to me

in the light of absence I pray all distance
become our one same house, stone chimney
in the light of burning wood, light
between syntax and intention,
light between how you excite me
and what I answer,
crimson light of expectation, in the soft
light of commercial arrangements, in the moneyed
light of pleasant restaurants in snowy suburbs, with ferns,

in the lesbian light that touches every woman,
in the light that finds you, in the orange
light of dissidence, lambda light, the ruddy
light they serve in catholic churches, in glasses,
in Mary light, blue light, in the brown
light of leather, of lore,
yellow flowers of woad light,

in the light of books you give me

in the light of your love understanding me
in the light of my darkness receiving—

And on the other end of the pier,
the part called Night,
there is a light now everybody knows
though everybody goes there and that light
is in every body. The knowers know
and the be-ers are.
Here the waves are sharp,
rims etched against the lower sky,
light carved into light,
intaglio light showing through in cloud,
amber light of rainstorm, crimson
light just before sunset, sideways light,

mother light that nothing sees
mother light that all forgives
mother light that wounds, or wounded light
meat light, Greek light,
eye light is skin light, light
of the oldest languages you speak,
low-waisted light, light of a belt around your waist,
light of silver thread in silk,
light around the earth, zone light,
house of tragedy full of comic light,
my arm around you light what do you see,

tree light snow light everything
washed away by that ocean they call Night now
I call it nothing it doesn't
see me it forgives my caress,
virgin light, palpable, pure
as a flag, pure as an unknown word

in an unknown language spoken by your mouth,

speak it, pure as my sleep, pure light
and North Sea coast light, pure
light and California light, light
of every street I've ever known,
light of every house and every car's light,

pain light, light inside bones broken or whole,
cheap light of understood ideas,
bad light of getting what I want, fierce
light of wanting, dear light of unknown roads,
light of someone at the door.

Melencolia

after Dürer

I.

Be near me then, it is only a design.
Only a door painted on the wall of your room.
Go in and out. It shows a man almost naked
whose folds and shadows are prussian blue
but whose flesh where the sun strikes it
is the color of raspberries in milk
an hour after immersion. Sugar. This
is the Theologian. He is falling from heaven.
For over a week his skin has endured
the facility of his descent. The soft
bronze hairs on his forearms are burnt off.
This earth his landing place is still a sunset off.

2.

What have I sacrificed. What is the arrow
that took my eyesight, shot
from inside my cranium out, yearning
for a world it pierced me to behold.
Listen. What was the tambourine

Sally clattered as she took off her skirt
in one wide unwrapping gesture meaning me
in? At the fifteenth degree of the sign
Saturn is exalted in Libra. Buildings
are understood, measurements are known,
people understand the frustrum of a cone
by formula. The music of an immense order
peoples our love. One by one
the numbers follow him down from heaven.

3.

All that matters is this meaning?
No. He falls
and what sustains us is the detail,
pores of the skin, the map
of all our difference.
I want to tell you simply that
his body Language is who falls.
When his body touches earth we leave the room
by the spontaneously self-enchanted door.

4.

Midafternoon the heat came back.
It was a farmer with his mate,
his son with a mattock ope'd the earth
and we were two, all of us two
and never one, no one.
Midafternoon the farmer
forgot to hear his Bruckner Eighth.
All those opalescent spaces

were actual places: he moved
within them and the earth closed.

5.

This is then what Saturn sent:
the golden age, the afternoon
between the beech tree and the lilac
in the place called Europe.
The endless books of the philosophers,
the bridges of Koenigsberg.
But most a sense that our palaver
feeds and is fed by a secret stream,
a simple current underneath the mind.
That is the mind.

Windows

Beware the simplicity of windows
that they show a landscape you will never
by the nature of things
be permitted to enter.

It is there
and you
(whoever and wherever you are)
are here.
Language keeps you in your place.

The hills endure your absence forever.

The Hunter

I must have thought I was a kind of hunter,
the way it was when I was a kid,
you got up real early and got dressed in the cold dark
quiet as you could, treating the bedroom
as if it already was a part of the forest
and any noise could drive them away, the way
you went down to breakfast and stared at the oatmeal
as if their hoofprints streaked across it
and you could tell the way they went, the way
you set out, all of the men of you, you were
somehow a man already, and stepped quiet
over your own land to the curtain of woods,
all of you side by side but spread out, all of you
holding rifles, all of you into the woods
and before the light was full someone fired
and you fired too but you fired into he air
and nothing was killed and later you all came home
and the next time they went out you stayed home
and they had become they and you had become you,

I must have thought I was a kind of hunter
that could track you through cities and memories
and raise the rifle of simple desire against you
and make you fall down and lie there and like it
the way hunters pretend the deer must like to die
since they do it so easy and so quiet.

From the Resting Place of the Grail

The clue to unbounded transmissions from the architects of space
Whose least doubtless afterthought this archipelago of suns and
Random jests of rock whereon we live most likely is

Is (a) bronzed shoulder bared intimating braless lushness near to
(b) wind from ocean stirring my back hairs or the (c) man
On his way to the beach seen now again at almost evening,

Paenecrepuscular, postnatatory, sinucumbent mass
Market paperback perhaps read no further in than outward bound,
Hoarse voices of tamed beach revelers, prisoners of the sun.

This archipelago of frail delights. There is a final message (flip
Open that stolen Gideon bible to a risky passage in Hosea)
Cloaked in the sweetest merest lodging of our flesh—

That Body is innocent, and on high. That Speech when it listens
Says everything. That Mind that knows itself knows all.
But you, you want to know the fuselage markings on some

Turbo saucer that brought our race to this planet, you
Want to know your father's name. Be ashamed. A body is enough
        to have.
Stand with me on Glastonbury Tor inside St Michael's roofless
        tower

And look up: the patch of sky you see is your real home. I also
Fell. Suppose our heads tilted up without effort, gazing
Our way beyond the blue veil. The clue falls from your hands.

Kiss me. My mouth is the lips of your mother before you were born.

A Flower for the New Year

At first I couldn't remember the name
of the vine borne flower that climbs
so scraggly up the south wall of my porch,
I see it now, bare and crazy looking, like a hank
of twine a cat got tired of bothering,
and that every spring you coax so carefully
into a few meager gorgeous deep purple blossoms,

but that we saw triumphantly tropical in the cold
rainy summer of St Barnabas Road in Cambridge,
how do they do it, the Smith's doorway and the yard
next door purple with them, visions of Persephone
and ancient excess, the wild half-unconscious
half-drunken wilful excesses of Greeks!

And then I remembered the name, clematis, and couldn't
remember if I'm supposed to say cle may tis or cle mah-
tis, like the man in the song about tomatoes
(you say, I say, let's call), anyhow, that flower,

and then I couldn't understand why I was worrying
about the names of flowers or the names of anything
or music or even the flower itself, Greeks and all
their purple antics, their raving gates and trances,
wild throats receiving and decanting seeds from

all the worlds above they meant by "Gods,"

and why should I be thinking about the gods or even winter
when there are men and women who have no homes
with or without flowers on the wall, men and women
who have no history except what happened to them
last night, in the street, when another man
or another woman, said, nameless, or did, motiveless,
this thing, what thing, gave, or took, or struck,
or in the common way of bleary midnight New Years misery
touched, just touched, and these, without a chair
or a floor to put it on, without a wall,

children only of the wind, who live in the weather
in the unromantic hate-winds of their appetite,
who suffer their own resentment more than their hunger,
whose pain is permanent, hence forgettable, always alone
but never lonely because every human being is their enemy
and a man fighting for his life has no time to be lonely,

and they fight, for their lives, in silence and squalor,
their stupefied eyes almost merry with glowering envy,
and I sit here baffled by the name of purple flowers,
remembering all the girls in my life as they step
naked-footed lewdly up the chill sedate corridors
of the marble museum of my heart, I worship their nakedness
while some man lies in the snow on Sixth Avenue with no shoes,

so dark the flower, shaped like a trumpet, darker
as I peek inside, or walk up down that curving bell
into the sound of what manner of sky they keep there,
who?, in the homeland of that flower whatever its name,
we do what we can and lie down in the dark, and what we cover
ourselves with against the wind is nobody's business,
so dark the flower, so dark the heavy traffic of names.

Horse

Waiting at the stable for the horse to be born
the Imperial Stables
with Lipizzaners toe dancing up the parvis
delicate hooves to make
small clods to rise and fall,
                              the earth
                    is a manner of dancing,
when will the last horse come?

The horse with the orange light in its eye,
the horse on fire, the calico horse,
the horse with the polished mirror bright aluminum rump
            mane of milkweed and dame's rocket tangled,
the horse with Latin teeth and Chinese heart,
the horse with his hoof in your lap
his wet muzzle annoying the nape of your neck wisely,
the horse with a grumbling belly the horse
with a crow on its head and a cat on its back
and the cat has blue fur, the horse of judgment,
a horse full of politics a horse full of new quarried stones
shining white in the sun, a horse
is waiting for you, his yard-long pole is
looking for you,

when will you arrive at the human destination,

when will the prefigured certainties dissolve into one
     spontaneous touch,
when will you let the last horse find you,

the horse with Roman nails stabbed into its withers,
the horse dripping with sun,
the horse whose shadow covers a dozen acres and whose cry
wakes you between midnight and dawn,

the horse with crazy eyes like a doting papa,
the horse with honey stuck in his throat
clearing his throat forever whence pure vowels are born among
     men
the horse upside down, the horse stuffed with silk and linen
     and books printed in Pali,
the horse at the barricades, the green horse who stumbles on
     the wind,
the big horse who remembers your mother, the horse
who makes you love your mother, the horse
with a telephone cord garlanded round his neck,
the horse who talks to the world suddenly and in a quiet voice
braying the truth of the matter, the horse in orange leaves,
the horse with horns on its head, on grass halms grazing,
the horse on sale in New Orleans, the old horse at the mill, the
     horse
dragging the barge on the Erie canal,
the horse a slave rides all night for weeks to the North,
the horse ramping a mare in Putnam County, a horse
who will never go back, a horse with three
exiles on his back escaping into the mountains,

when will you remember your liberty,
when will you let the green horse come,
last of a thousand horses, the horse that's here even now, right
     now,

has never been elsewhere,
the horse in your cellar, the horse on your roof,
the horse in your kitchen huger than sunlight,
the horse who sleeps standing up, whose eye
stares out of your navel, the horse in your bone,
the horse with the head and hooves of a horse,
the horse running towards you on the avenue of light,
the horse that was the first thing I saw when I died?

Afterdeath

I.

Coming back to my place
my place coming
into a place a place
is what holds
together the breath
of it goes out and comes
in the breath of it
is always returning

2.

So I find back
to a place to find
what is mine
what is coherent
as a color is
when it is a wave
behaving a house
behaving in time
is that it a place
without interruption

3.

And mine could be a tower
held tight in air
the insertion
of one person in another
a person in a place
a summons answered
the wind came first
I have no right
to the body I am

4.

To come back to no
situation orphan house
a child is the same
something coming close to itself
I knew the shape only
of what it was to hold
bodiless the liquid place
to be alone is not the same
I am not the same as myself
only by losing that place found.

from Ariadne: [*the first part*]

Dear Ariadne,

the womb is full. Black tufts of autumn corn sag under the
weight of their damp silk. It springs up as my foot settles, down
in, everywhere, grassy mud. Womb happening hour, speak my
baby for me,

I mean my body,

this piece of farmer, meek silo lofted, sleek money, hum, drum,
valve of the day sluiced clean, hum of sun in the corn stob, hum
of wind in stubble, sum of yearnings, touch,

touch!

Christ hears you from the dead, valve of Easter, lich gate of
the tomb, broken barrier, bound over boundary, steep
deciding, comes,

comes to town.

Do you hear all the things I am trying not to say?

Never is a sumptuous music, isn't it, more like Bruckner
than Brahms,

bring me a glass of water, pour it in my lap.

Say: here I reverse the agon and the aion, both at once,
here I transverse the ancient flow,

Water of spine water of life cold by conjure swear by

I baptize thee stainless, woman.
So saying, look me home into the paradise
we keep for each other, lakely, neat in each our faces.

•

Are the soundings in feet or fathoms,
Men or women
Drowned to approach you

Over the drone of seas

How cool you are, clear,
Born after storm

" 'I am full' means 'I am pregnant,' " you said, and the car
slewed a little to the right, cars can't hear quotation marks

Map you sent
Feet or fathoms
Miles or message

Solve these numbers
Pick the thread of them
Out of all the million
Million threads in all her weaving

Homer to Ariadne:

Think of all those poets, or these poets, the lyric ones, the ones
who are brief and tuneful:

They won't have the least idea. Or all they'll have will be *idea,*
not a trace of substance,

>   the animal
>   I followed
>   all my life
>   through so many thickets
>   and slew on the white sand
at last and the sea was always egging me on.

They will not know, these poets to come, lost as they are in their
little poems, their will to be short, and sweet, and go to sleep,

they will not know. They will make fragments of fragments, cast
shadows of a fake ego, make an echo shout.

Look at any line of mine and you'll see a dozen of their small
poems waiting, *breathing there quietly, waiting,* waiting for the mind's
body's chest's breath's heart to release them,

a dozen you'll find, easy, and in my whole work
uncountable myriads.

Look at a line like _____

•

and Homer couldn't find the line the line
he meant or of the myriads he meant

lay quiet in the fallow of his mind,

burnt brown and grown a little back
sweet under May fog, cool drizzle

couldn't say the line he meant the meaning
faltered under the bleak apple trees
unhinged for spring, with blossoms
sub-odorous, with pale rose tips to petals,

until he thought the whole world round him was the line
he meant,
I wrote all of this he said
and thought he said no more than I wrote this.

[*the Opera:*]

Cold rain and happy drizzle trees
a mist veil let slip

the vanity of creatures that I am
o mirror me long,
quicksilvering night cloud,
against your opaque honesty
I read my face.

Fates. An arquebus or cross-bow stretch't,
something old, aimed
long ago, the bolt
let fly, long ago, finds me now—

o there is arthritis in the world

and answering
and being vague and high colloquial of praise,

how can you let your body ache
                              I pose
                              this music
as music,
                     poise peas on knife tip even
to nibble before opera
reeling,
                     blanched bone of my shirt cuff
in half-light suddenly shown.

Shone. This was the first act:
Now see
             in pain herself outstretch'd upon a Rock,
hear her lover idling up the straits
get wind of her
                       (the sea bruit, sea
vague, sea holler,

                           hallows him on)
and all his little intellect
must strive to this
so not-so simple
                      strand, whoosh of surf
on shingle,
               to arrive.

In pain he found her
(founder in the shoals, mere man,
try to lift
the weight of her in your eyes, the glory
stored for you in her hips)

arthritis of the mind, a truth-ache,
nightscare, were-crow, lye-a-bed-ease,
some bad sick, can't her and leap rosies,

all those she flew)

till he on smite-rock smote
and by the say-rock spoke:

>Ari my lioness lonely lying
>lie on this my me,
>Adnai my mistress liege lovely
>be my siege my empery

and all such boyistries he babbled
                nor did she wake.

Not yet, not to such wordage bound
—and all he meant to say was "I am nigh."

And he was night, so the third act began,
tocking of tam-tams and outrageous ordinaries,
a splinter of sense off some pinging triangle
and then the flab of orchestra o'erwhelm'd

the frail safe-conduct of the melody.

Flimsy book! Portage perilous!
Unhand my omnibus, you cloud,
                and let me carry her.

But she is the property of her own mind, that *God*,
and will in her own time incarnate
Herself as Him to rescue her.

320   *from* ARIADNE (1991)

Torrents of applause and major thirds,
and thus an end make to your Grand Uproar.

And now we are quiet on the streets outside,
hand in hand remembering each other.

Now that the opera is over it is sweet. In Strauss's magnificent
opera within an opera, *Ariadne auf Naxos*, the early summons of
the Baroque is heard—Barock, the Germans spell it—casting
its spell on the early twentieth century, Busoni first, his Bach
transcriptions, then Strauss's love of Mozart, then finally
Stravinsky, imposing/posing his cool baroque, pre-baroque
harmonic locutions on our suffering age. So the language of the
Opera section of this letter, this is a letter, to you, Ariadne, you
who are and aren't she, who, she, the Lion Lady, the Tamer of
the Proud, the Lady of Beasts, she who on Naxos and in her
loneliness, approached by so many males, but so few who knew,
know, the power and energy of that fire to which, feebly and
goopily and sloppily, they aspire, try, try to come to, forget,
wander boyishly off, meaning no harm, traipsing off to the
Next—boys always move to the Next—the next who is, also,
in her measure, you. Who is not you. Only you are you, and
like a dandy slain with eau de violettes, some dreadful
Montesquiou prancing in Versailles, I do not dare to say your
name.

Your name is Ariadne, and you are you.

So the music (=language) of the opera is baroque. There is air.
There is color, mostly pale blue-green, like the appointments of
the monastery church of St Gallen. There is space. But the
language has to be teased from inside itself, a tickle in the ass, a
slight but persistent runny nose.

Running noise, her lovers fleeing. I am afraid of women. Only the sea consoles me in the extremity of commitment to which I have at length come. So many commitments. So many meetings.

Meat. He runs from his body, which he recognizes despite the artful way the gods have disguised it. That is his body on the spit slowly turned over the coals in the restaurant window in Chicago, South Halstead, Greektown, that is his body being hacked by the monk on a chopping block, chips of cow shank and cow meat flying off the shambles, still mostly tree stump, on a hillside in the Himalayas. That is his body close inside the reddening lobster shell, stifling in the steam released from the sea-weed it's packed in, inside the big blue enamel pot that sinister small sky. That is his body with the gaping yellow teeth pronging out of the brown dogshit colored unwrapped mummy in the case at the British Museum, a smelly rainy day the stink of old men in their woolen suits, the smell of mummy, my meat.

To the exact measure of my love for you I have been fleeing. Your tongue spoke inside my mouth: *Be afraid!* I am so afraid of falling in love with you.

And Homer laughed,
to see such deedless passions,

traits of mind
traits of union,

such quarrelsome joinings,

for a man's mind

to find a woman
like an arrow killing a deer,

folly upon folly
welded,

and the woman wanting it!
And women wanting men,

that is the funniest of all,
that cast away as she is,

in fact abandoned, she still
wants another one, some other one,
one of those, that kind, that
gender of betrayal

to come to her now
and speak to her tenderly
and mean what he says.
Alas, Ariadne, he can

only mean what he wants,
a man can only mean what he wants—
and Homer laughed
at his own heart crying,

at his own heart hungry
for every seabird he heard
screaming through that invisible sky
to the one place Homer

divided as he was
could never come,

come home.
For he came from many
and to many he returns.
A word spoken
in a crowd, a name
not clearly spoken, barely heard.

Prince Andrei Looks at the Sky

It is huge and full of difference.
He calls it endless, or without end.
Broad and solemn, like a midnight mass
except it's afternoon and men are dying,
not being born. Everything he ever saw
is suddenly much less interesting
than this almost nothing he's looking at
now, nothing, nothing but this.
The difference is called cloud, and in its
own language it is womanly, full of shawls,
iridescent silken cashmere, shawls and dances,
slow dances. What does he owe this brightness,
what can a man give to the sky? *A cock to one*
spoke I know it, orgy of Western awe,
suave summer's new tact, cock arbor, shall
new tact? Cock maybe, shall I,
crystally trellis? Soft some
new tact falls out of black, pen's poet moving.
So come you, be shown each
known new neighbor . . . But the prince is wounded,
the wound is worded, the words say this.
He bleeds the way the sky once so long ago
torn by a stone knife wielded, bled us.

Set on War

The fifteenth of January 1991 is the last day of the eleventh
month in the Tibetan lunar calendar; of this date it is said:
"night when the fates of those to die in the coming year are
decided."

Night when the fates are decided.
I turn into you. A fish
turns into the sea. The meaning
changes. We say it turns.

In front of the market they have tethered
a flock of little pigs.
People look at them uneasily, thinking
These are going to die to feed us.
Or *They*
have passions too, penises and personalities,
passions and no choices. They have no choices.

Thinking like that, people pass by the great bronze
pig at the gate of the market
near which squealing pinky blacky whitey pigs are stored,
people go inside the sheds and look at oysters
(*they have no choices*) artichokes and carrots
(they have no passions), artichokes unfolding
around a sweet and secret center,

way of Yantra, magic diagrams and concenters,
rule of thumb and plucks the palest satisfaction
out and be your lover. Be your dinner.

Sawdust shuffles underfoot
fishgut sheen, silence of the about to eat.
Choose me, all the dead salmon say,
turn my silver to your bronze insides

so I become you, my little weekend in a human form.

•

It was your year and you got all mixed up
with a star but at least you got to live in the sky

and the chestnut horses
of Brooklyn policemen
regularly begin lines with weak words then mount to the crux
where the horses stand on the bridges

over our heads! under their placid riders.
Do it but don't do it long
or leave him listening to his old Coltrane records
with his hand full of composting leaves,

it rains in the stars,
numbers are the bones of someone
you try to forget all your life

who looks at you in sunset windows
knees of horses airless skinny trees of obsolete oases go.

•

Every building every thing you need
a war begun today
busy against life
a woodpecker
inside a tree

Animals are only members of it
telephone river raft Penikese Island

the happiness we're desperate to forgive
overnight melted snow seeps into the cellar
by noon the sump pump will be needed, throb
surge of it comes on.

               The lover
sits on the side of the bed and takes off his shoes
she is getting less dressed in the bathroom
steam rising from the basin. I know that face
the devil in the mirror with green eyes

does she see too. The suspect.
I know we have to separate—

I'm not talking to you—I know these words enact
nightly their own history.

His socks her sleek pajamas he loves to touch
with middle and index finger tips
just where the blue satin dips to meet her delve.
Geography—who made this island?

Do you believe in trees, Gods, pencils
marriage as the union of opposites

like ink and paper? A body
is the opposite of what it eats

a flag is the only enemy of the sky.

Reading Li Shang-yin: Falling Flowers

Even you shaking myself out of the dust
of all I need you
    the differences, the terrible birds
you have quit my high pavilion
        the shadow of you
the shadow of me being
      so many days a complicated darkness
down there *in the garden*
      down there where the terrible shadow we were
is stepped on now by those birds, so awkward they are,
princes of the air clowns on the ground
preposterous feet
      the shadows come down to us only, sometimes,
     as this morning, of course missing you,
  not only you, not only me
 missing you,
     a shadow missing a part of itself, the dingy
quality the light has when it has no shadow to cast or
long waisted low slung
      you have come towards me
  equal to being born in aspect
of engagement,
    after the clandestine espousals
  of life with death
    they called the blue flower

in no one's hand,
                        how sumptuously you stretched
            on my couch

                        every muscle a remembering,
by truth to rouse,
                        or ruse, or lull, or con
            the Great Reader into highly specific acts of Oblivion,
our life is his amnesia.   Smooth of the hip
            socketed in the cup of the hand,
                                    the weight of,
                        a pendulum closeness
            to the gravid earth *below*
                                    to be born inside
finity where the *flowers* grow—
                                    whose color are they?
                        meek by dint of memory
astir in fire?
                        Writing to track what reading has in mind.
Scattering on your breast
the petals of wantfulness,
                                    the blue tone snug so deeply
            in the red
                        so that the sunset
                        knows you,
                        you here among the eternity of conversations
and so few of them wet   tongue-tip to your
                                    quiet breast,
                                                a garnet
                        holds that color also
                                    to the base of your spine, a current
            the women of old spoke
                                    to their sons a little bit

and to their daughters much,
                              language,
                          language of the *west*
lewd grammars of a nomad people,
                          for in my thought I have caressed
              the sacred geomantic precincts of your body
my hands heavy with grease
                          from just such alien sheep. Wool pull,
          flowers nibbled, not bright animals
hoofing through your garden, your air,
                                  I hear the crows
                  adventuring the little left
                          after life the silver snow
              to them
          in a full moon time
is given,
              I wait for you, comfort of your body beside me
          as if suddenly an old man inside me
                                  strung with that yearning
              to pluck tone
                      song
          as from the bones of the body sounded
                  and all our torture just that music
          muscle,
                  wound, sound, wound,
      the knell of beast comfort moving
      to take possession of this carrion mind,
                                  clearing,
              like a procession of Grail knights
          disappearing, violet line into falling snow fading,
and yesterday I saw the garden wall, old bluestone slabs,
the shale cut to slates, the marble steps
                  broken, all broken, brick wall
          bent under the bare lianas of wisteria, the root stocks

twisted in cold evening, all lilac
                              was the east then
                    across the whole little world
            from that setting sun
                              fallen past the hemlocks,
the contra-sera even-pale,
                              isolate woodpecker also
                    from before us *flown along the* river of air
        they apprehend (we don't)
                              we know not that we know not,
                                        base metal
                    we have scotched our gold with,
                                        endured with
            cunning when we might have thrived with openness
exulting,
            o it is not nothing
                    to have a red flower on my windowsill
            in such weather,
                              whose many petals, still red, dry
and fall
                    onto the blue tile kitchen floor,
                                        and to crush
                    gently enough one leaf of it
            releasing
from flexile structure one scent of *form*,
                    as from the *twisted dike* of matter a leak of sense.
To smell a geranium
        in winter
            is better
than all the bergamot
        of the Midi,
            be with me
though
        to savor it.

I want your side
to me, my hand
between your thighs
escorting
the warmth of you,
after,
into sleep.
Dusk. We have *passed into distances*
of each other, swayed in blue ferryboats
across bitter cold straits,
and there was always
someone near us, a bravo smoking cigarettes, and that too
virginia was a kindness to remind.
Compassion.   Compassion,
in the faded light, I reach for your return
who never left me,
the world
is not made of partings,
brass farthings,
she goeth forth
with her sweetie
to endure
these new
winter nights
with brainless screwing

but the separations
of which I am master
are far other,
it is a matter (a scatter)
of the metals
cinnabar and copper
and what is left of me
when love absterges

        the newsworthy patinas
your kisses left
    and everybody knows it
        I am your man,

and so in faded light I ask her, she is my colors, I reach
for where she is and where she's going
                and on the phone Joan tells me
        how Lana has run off with Erica
                midwinter, Tivoli disaster,
    pale fiancées of a wanton star.
            I reach I reach
    my life
is all about reaching
                into wherever it is dark, wherever, wherever,
and listen! the children
    of the night! their music!
                    I tell her, Dear one, reach
for her return. She tells me: I will never
take her back,
            for all her cheating
        was a wound
            in the flesh of my *time*, and time
    that heals all else, has no way to heal itself—
                our years she took
        six years
                and spent them,
                    this is our winter's tale,
lukewarm tea and shiny petals of our polaroids
        torn up and scattered on the floor
                before the dead fire in the hearth,

and when we love
    what thing is left

that shapes the shadows

even of our house,
        so that doorway
            in it
is only about her coming through?
        I have torn
            the images
of the life she tore
        and still can't bear
            to sweep them away.

Patmos

A bible dissolves in upon itself a man renews
feeble breadstuffs what does a woman do
she goes back to San Diego she reads philosophers
under sunblock 25 the island
—an island is always imaginary, grisaille,
full of wise donkeys old men who remember baseball
orange trees the sweet clementines hang in your neighbor's
garden
salt o such salt—
when the book opens a man is born.
                              I don't know
what a woman is.
                    When a book is closed
the heavenly Jerusalem hurries down
lawyers give up alcohol, from the heights of Rancho Maguey
a transhumance sets in—uneasy citizens in German cars
decamp for colder cities. Adversity is coming,
meet it halfway. I, Jacob, saw a globe
descend from heaven, or was heaven. I was heaven.
He held it out to me, my master, and said *Inhale*
this universe; if you must breathe, breathe this, this large
designless fabric of the mind, this hopeless joy
this now, he said and offered it, my master did,
I took and like one suckling sucked it in,
the glassy air of one small blue planet

and all the déjà-vus beyond it, wheel upon wheel.

And he gave me bread, fierce bread, from the ovens
of the gods, those earls and grand dukes of this feud
I mean this muscle called music, other way round,
I mean the world. I, Jacob, did breathe in.
And they said, in Whitman's way, "Élève,
you have said all this before!" and I, not abashed,
confessed, "Yes, how shall a thing be so
that is not said? Or being said
not said again? Does the wind speak only once?

And have I not seen this sun before?
Life is redundancy, fish eggs and overmeasure pour!"
They slunk back to their manuals and magazines,
and left me blue-balled with urgent messages
I step delicately you-ward, now, to inscribe in you
waving my calmed hands through the sleepy air
of Patmos! the preposterous island
of the previous, whose sturdy wisdoms are all windows
framed with the wood of orange-trees, salt-bleached, sweet
with the darting shadows of ortolans, witty
as hummingbird tongues on the great Cuzco–San Diego Flyway
heavy, heavy, sheep & shadow, heavy sugar, deft metabolites,
sugar of the dead, gateau with such precious jam,
white-eyed, terrorized by heaven, handful of jewels
all raspberry and currant, Saint Johannes berries
in our days come down)
                              a man must be strong
to break bread on an island, his breakfast bread
break what she hands to him barely awakening
half of her still drowsy with cormorants
deep-shouldered in the black bay.

Mapping

A book for us to write, like this:
you'll uncap the pen and hold the barrel
you'll press the iridium nib against soft paper
you'll draw a line—extend
it to a word
it will run from your hip up your heart to your hand
and it will say.

And what do I do. I sit beside you and turn the pages.
Diminuendo then sudden fortissimo—
I know where I am in the world by loudness alone.

How will the book know when we write it
what it's supposed to say.
It says what it must say.
It is a single piece of paper, very large or infinite,
and everything has to be findable there,
metabolism of desert rodents,
ratio of fat to muscle in singing birds,
predators, swallowers of discarded flesh.

•

A man is bent double over the hood of a car
and the police are twisting his thick sunburned arms behind
        his back

putting handcuffs on.
Ambulances with swinging lights, sheriffs and troopers
and a street full of frightened people.

This has to be in the book. This is the map.
It has to show the fear, it has to show my hand
squeezing your wrist too hard, the doubt
beginning to show in your eyes as you look at me,
the grief in mine that I would twist the world again,
that I'm doing it again, hurt you to love me.
That I can't trust the world to come to me and stay.
Draw me this world I don't trust, draw me trusting it.

Hot thunder. Show me.
I am a man bent low
constrained by circumstance,
why is it so sad,
where does this grief come from
you hear in my voice,
what do I know that makes me grieving,
I grieve with an ancient remorse I don't understand,
draw me a map with me remembering, forgiving, with me
        letting go.
Thunder. Dark thunder. Dark hot thunder.
Light is full of conveyance.
Oh that was lightning, it touched you faintly.
Lit up the profile of my face like a flicker of remorse.

•

They all are, all are speaking,
petals   copper acetate   old names
of a sweet old chemistry
loving things with language
               that now we only know by number

a celadon vessel tinged nudely with palest crimson
shaped like the square root of five.

•

Map our revelation.
When you decide where the mountains are
we can find the Grail Temple
thickening clouds over the grain elevator
a scrap heap and the gates
swing open out of solid gold

hands around your hips now squeezing too tight
what is between Chicago and the North Pole
you squirm in my hands
trying to get free trying to get closer to me
how will I ever know
I hold so tight
I crush all the old maps in my hands my strong
hands give me a new map draw me a mountain

how strong you make me
draw me a map of your root honesty lend it to me
measure it all the way back to the moon

this map now
we begin

I think with your hand

you feel your body press down,
Lex dead of AIDS and David's friend
and ——— dying of it,
the pressure talks up the prussian blue of your veins

until you draw the map
complete in all its rivers copses spinneys
                man-built weirs
        copper mines   salt pans
        dotted lines for caves
                        bearing down and in
from staggering cliffs
you mark by a bundle of contour lines
    —always 57° down there
        inside the constant earth
                midnight in San Francisco the cry of men

map the cry of them
desperate for your body all of your bodies

until you draw the map
                with every bight cove fjord quarry
        all the Ragusas of dubious argosies
    jabbering lighthouses staining the dark

until you draw the map
                with every battle site pricked out with crossed swords
        the Christian ruins and the man of war
                        sunk in the harbor
                fouled anchors oil rigs spirit guides
        marking ley lines with eye chalk

until you draw the map complete
        with an old woman in Appleton
                eating cheese on saltine crackers

this book of ours will not be finished, draw it
it is the only book,

I am waiting for your map
to forgive me
to explain the silence of the world,

draw a mesa and a bed
a snake asleep on sandstone cold morning
draw hemlocks in Russia
draw the Vatican if there is one
a Pope legislating from the star Canopus
draw the men haunting the corridors of ancient buildings
draw the shadow the moon casts on the Plaza de Toros
    when all the drunks have come home
and the bull is bleeding to death outside the wooden wall

then draw the shadow the moon throws down on the earth
no one can see
but we feel it
hard on our shoulders
sometimes when we turn
to each other or look
the same way in the sky.

What way is that? How does the land know
what the map is making it do?
Which way does a word point
when we look through each other
whoever we are?
                And it goes there,
nobody's listening, let the word go,
let the map pour out of your hands
hurry,
        you know something you almost remember.

ཨ

Startled by a sentence I find written
in Charlotte's hand, in Tibetan, on the table—

from the beautiful white letter A, the wisdom treasure is born.

What is born from letters?
Joey holding his mother's hand all through
her labor on the birthing stool to bring forth
(6:52 A.M., 2 September 1992, Loudonville NY)
Miles Roger René Joris-Peyrafitte

who holds the letters by the hand

draw them from the sky

But the sky is mind, isn't it?
        pronounced *inn'it?*
                Inuit, Innana,

                                        the sky
is just down these stairs,
turn left at the bottom of your heart,

                                                Bauch,

a belly waits for a princess.
From the Intelligential Heaven

344   *poems* (1991–1993)

a mother wit ascends.

From the beautiful white letter
                            (I'm trying to renew
the charge, the battery is dead,
                so eat the battery
        like a Babylonian,
                            the Kingdom
of Heaven is like unto a rod
                buried end-down in earth,
it casts a shadow
by which most men tell the time
a wise man pulls it out and hides in it a secret place)

But the words are always telling
telling, the cruel teacher comes along (as in *Louis Lambert*)
and rips up the boy's philosophy,
the word he came to earth to speak
                           (in fear of writing,
           dark Socrates, stand
       in the doorways all your hours,
                  breathe the sense of it,
        don't speak)

                  his poem,
his heart-habit strivings
to declare
        what isn't there.

    There is a beautiful
      letter in the air.
        I see it time after time,
            and all I see besides

gets born, Aleph, from that sign,

Aleph or Abel, slain into speech.

(I'm trying to renew
that color on the tree,
                          the Kingdom of Heaven
may be likened to a book
                          of blank pages
            on which the sunlight falls
                          casting the shadow of a leaf or leaves
a child's finger traces
                          idly
                                    the Kingdom
of Heaven may be likened to idleness.

All I know now
I knew at seventeen
from the laze life,

all the rest
is just experience
to order or purpose.

There is silence
                          (the battery is dead

in heaven
                          (I left the map in your heart)

for half an hour
                          (wind the clock).

The beautiful bank teller

moves white teller fingers
back and forth over money
musically

in the magic high and low of counting

to me what is mine
from me what is everyone's

silence earned,
     Pound
among peacocks,
insufflator breathing fingerprint powder
over scant evidence of the attention we paid

(the Kingdom of Heaven is like a book we read and forget)

Our Lady of the Hours
who are you
keeping track of us from St John's Church

what is born from power
settles so calmly
into the meek alchemical afternoon

(reading books, taking powders, tea)
that without turning our Will to it

a person desired comes to our scapegrace door
and we let in

counting all the wiles
of Gideon and Joshua

until the courthouse reels
overwhelmed with such innocent testimony
—all fantasy—

spiders living in the drawer

a book taken out in moonlight and publicly beaten
—hear the thumps and thwacks of the bailiff's staff

until the heart of language
lists its haunch (ventricle) hard against the wall.

Hear me, I was man.
I had a pride commensurate with my shadow at evening,
an appetite equivalent to Arcady.
Then I was stone.

                    Shepherds scratched
                    their easy avowals on me
and I have repeated through every age
the simplistic lovesongs they made me wear,

the Kingdom of Heaven is like a ball
a child tosses into the sky that does not come down,

they thought I understood the words I say,
but I am all saying, just saying
                    I am the hand holding your hand
          and making you strong
                    as I can
          while you say
                    what you have to say,
thus the Kingdom of Heaven may be likened also
          to rowdy
peasants drinking stolen champagne just over the crest of a hill.

The Phantom of the Opera

1. *Following Evening*

It is like a carriage. It runs away over the crest
of a hill you never really know is there
until you have to walk up it, you find
yourself there, it is summer, mid-afternoon,
and the sun lies on you, judgment and decree
and no hope. The terrible island of the body.
No escape from that. You move west
as best you can, following evening
into the cave five catacombs beneath the earth
where the king of dragons questions closely
every drop of water on the earth
and hears what all beings are doing, even
what they think in their secret nightmare
lusts, their bank accounts of merciless fears.
You too are inquired of by that subtle voice
that hisses like the radiator in your aunt's apartment,
the one who died one December day in her
brother's arms, whispering of the mysteries
of the Rosy Cross she feared had failed her.
Her brother was your father, of course,
your feet were too big, it had always been too hot
and Paris was full of people you didn't desire.
To go to the world and not want what you find!

2. *Mysterious Barouche*

It was waiting. Is everything waiting?
She is an exile and the axle broke.
Seized at Varennes, she had little
life left in her, she and her husband
who survived that operation on his penis
only to be factored beneath a bigger knife.
Or do I have the wrong king? Wrong kind
of mercy, to remember some bright details
of history and not have a single
friend to be good to, when all men are kind to me.
All I ever needed was to be honest to you,
you with the lake behind you and all that dying done
come back now with a smile in your aspiration
meaning to forgive your lumbering Lancelot
the thirty-three degrees of his infidelity,
riding in an ox cart indeed, among cauliflowers!
Deeper in mystery, the black carriage lurches
away from the Opera. No one is in it.
We are waiting for the aspiring soprano
to finish the highest, gentlest, of all her notes
and carry her sordid paramour to heaven.
No devil wants him. The devil is too busy
using men's desires to decode the world,
a world strictly unappealing to His Majesty
the Devaputra ever-Mara lordly liar,
king of the rodent whimsy that rules all life.
Henchmen beat the unattractive aesthete to death
and toss his body in the river where he comes from.
Source of all her art and majesty the humect flow
beneath the pavement of her simple schoolgirl lusts
and all the simplistic fervors of her audience,
to hear, and by hearing understand! What nonsense

this, by such a man deemed worth dying for?
This was music, and it alone renewed the earth.

3. *I have heard his voice, Raoul*

Yet there have been evenings when I heard his voice
indistinguishable from yours or from the Buddha's voice
speaking as it does so often from the ground, Merlin
or some jack crow who waits for meat along my lawn.
I woke up worrying about the French word *gazon*
supposed to mean plot of natural grass. But the opera
is all Astroturf and riddles, styrofoam palaces,
dreams that fold back firmly to the dominant and sleep.
But underneath the building there are streets
and underneath the streets the Fact of Life continuous
from universe to universe, leaping all the gaps or chaoses
any number of philosophies propose to daunt my love
or keep us from murmuring our *toujours, toujours!*
The ghost voice is the only one that tells. By voice alone
we built our boulevards and chose cathedrals
to lift the carven gargoyles in the air, newts of fire and air,
Nagas lifted into the permanence of space, the merciful,
the uninflected. I have heard his voice all my life in fact,
as fact, the only certainty. This voice taught us to sing,
and by singing understand. Dragons hoarding eggs
beneath the earth. Wise women scorning to possess.
Emeralds and ottomans, a groaning harmonium
keyboard lit by tallow candles made right here on the ranch—
how could you fail to love me, you taught so well?

Satyr Mourning a Nymph

I suppose the most beautiful painting in London is Piero di Cosima's Satyr Mourning a Nymph. It is in the National Gallery, and there is a dog in it. The image seems to ask the following questions:

Is she wounded or is she dead or does she sleep?

Who did it, if it was done?

In the far distance, right, behind the pack of dogs, we see the west end of Cuttyhunk Island. Bartholomew Gosnold's tower is clear exalted in the lucid evening. At its base Caliban is offering one more unwelcome sacrifice to Setebos.

The satyr is mourning, yes, but his face is full of wonder, full of that kind of almost clinical curiosity we often find in twi-natured beings, centaurs, aegipans, and the like. He seems to be thinking, through his grief: So this is death, this is the thing that mortals always suppose shapes or abrupts their little lives. Am I a mortal too? Will I one day enter this curious tender stupidity that seems now to hold my love?

And will there be someone to ponder at my side when I, for the first time in all my life, no longer have the sense to answer?

But all round him as he thinks his grief through the light is busy answering.

Voyage to the Center of the Earth

Knowledge is not a matter of it—
two traveled Woden pillars jettisoned
will light the way—the way wood
burns deep in water—to our new islands
where Retribution touches the delicate coast.
It is a ship that beats against you.

It is an idea. New icelands.
The small can be a word
a word doesn't have to be heard
to be a word, doesn't either have
to say to be heard. Hearing is seldom.

So when the weather bends to look at you
to see the seacoast green behavior of your eyes
remember to be small. You listen
if at all to the basalt of its basement,
the bottom things, dark characters
who strangely know your language
and greet you mornings saying *I know what you dreamed.*

Can you forgive us all? We
who were your alphabets. Can you be wrong.
The shadow comes from the sun,
without it we do not know our way.

Whoever we are. Let the beam go now,
let it fall into the deep Buxtehuding billow
off a little northern coast that's always you.
Most of the birds fly off you step ashore.
Here build your temple, you have finished with the gods.

A cormorant stays. A gull up there gores the sky
and you think you hear your own old wounds cry out.
And there the grey smooth silence lacerates itself
you cry. Let it be as if I never hurt you, could you?
Let it be as if the island never fell
up from the bottom of the vandal sea, and all these
volcanoes never spoke this word now grown so hard.

Stone law, unforgiving of that first abuse,
the fire flows from yearning. Stone law.
Once love fails you it always does. Save us
from going through the door or sinking
into the nonsense of that forgiving fire. Father
gone, mother gone, nothing but a name you have
and that lives only in other people's mouths.
No matter how many names you have how can you
say yourself, and if you did would you listen?

And when in this journey the wind bends you forward
to study the map you mounted by the binnacle
to show the new shapes the earth gives to my despair
what does the map see when it looks up at you
and searches with its mindless kindly thing-light
the deep anxiety of every human eye? What do eyes do
while we read? The distractions haunt us,
we wake with an old prayer in mind, as mind.
And those natives staring at us, birds or witches,
the thick dark mothers half-compassion and half-rock,

waiting to hurt us into life. Why is it so hard?

One reading the map. One standing in the sky. One animal
who was always there. This is the voyage
to the center of the earth—*I tell you a secret consolation:*
she is Emanation. Faithful heart of the phantom,
sweet friction that lies to feed the empty wind
and make it our actual fire. Practice of the heat,
the road down. Smoke of fumaroles, a field of hurt,
the beak of Iceland tearing at my heart. I saw it once—
how hard we have been hurt, an island you.

We are tired of all this liberty. You bend forward
into the wind of information, you read like a prisoner
tearing through a wall with his fingers, words
you break to find the secrets of, daylight in the folds.
All science comes through this ill-fitting door.

The Triads

I.

Things disappear. A suite
of music from *Don Juan* by Mozart.
And then they dare

to play a flute concerto by Herr Quantz.
Measures measuring nothing,
roads going

not at all.
These are the triads of Britain
beginning,

this is the wood and this is the island
to which we come
again and again when Troy burns down,

middleweight masochistic joggers
springing dog-wise into the trees
and this is the flute

to which they dance
this modern sense
of owing something to yourself

the world is coaxed to bring
by acts of self-destructive reverie
on roads. In rain.

With pain
we live again.
I have no evidence

except as much as Taliesin did
leaf-mold and lizard bones
slipping through my nerveless fingers

to say it all again
what has never been spoken
from the first star-fall on this world till now,

this burning argument
love used to coerce our lingering
unsheltered on the appalling slopes.

A flute has nothing much to say
except this little thing:
when I speak they have to listen.

2.

The music is not bad
except as music is.
Filling the space of time we know

we have so far to go
to find the core or crisis of the forest
that stretches without interruption

to the bleak matinees of the mountains,
the proprieties
from which we were escaping

are there before us. The chapel
full of horses, the horse
with no eyes, the snake skeleton

forming a figure eight on the paving stone
there at the crossing of the nave
where lovers stand to swear their futures

twisting and untwisting
this meek infinity
we give each other with our yesses.

The chapel.
In this forbidden information
everything you'll ever need

stands before you masked as your dream.
You think it's night.
You think you're sleeping.

     3.

Troy town
the towers
spill their shadows

town their spirals
writhe through the dry earth
shadow of water

in a dream of fire
Maeander Scamander the river
turning,

Troy town came here
in our heads the language
twisted round,

the adjective before the noun,
the verb before the subject
whispering in forest logic

the glade
where languages are made,
the town

which is made of hunger.
And hunger built a house
of many streets

and sent its young men
out to sell their time its young
women out to sell their future,

and in the turning
the street too turns round
and bites the house,

the house falls down
around its man
and then the child again

is a citizen of trees.
In Corbenic a shadow writhes

in the fire light of burning Troy.

In Michigan a fall of snow
hides the first wound.
Under his slow footsteps

(the leg is mending now,
the dog companionable
in shabby woodlots near the highway)

you hear the shield clangor,
the earth-word spoken
beneath the hasty laws.

4.

The smell of our roses
answers the deep places
where the words began,

Nodens lives there
his head asleep in sea wrack
his body wide awake

until the ocean sleeps
the smell of any flowers
understands us

like chalk cliffs gleaming
just after rain
when the sun has set

beyond the valley

and the last baking
is finished and the bread

is cold and the tables
not even the flies
expect anything from the tables

and the roses
we know
know us

this recent flower
of our scarlet
attentions

how many societies
exiles revolutions
it took to make a rose

no simple song
the cultivars
these Persian messages.

So sea
in our heads
and roses on the table

I hope you live with
me forever
isn't that what the birds

those fidelities
insist on every morning
to remind?

Crow in a tree
we do not know
what anything is saying,

we make it up
listen,
Taliesin is just listening

until each thing
confesses
its secret name

known before now
only to the wind,
tree semaphore

thorn anthems golden cosseted
dusty pronged evangelists
shouting pollen pollen in the night.

Man Sleeping

for Charlotte

He had been sleeping for an hour and the ocean changed
he had been dreaming towers and the sand stretched west
trying to enlist him in one more continent.
Elephants and equipoise. Market towers, minarets.
They wanted his sleeve full of doves
and his desires must be delicate as frog spawn
dry in the noon time heat.
He wanted nothing of what they wanted of him,
slept again like the barque *Unparalleled*
ran aground off this shoaly island
full of bibles and Dutch cheese and gabardine.
Red skulls of it wedged in rocks for weeks
till gulls and weather woke him
reeling from the Carpenter's embrace
—whose tongue was talking so fast in his mouth?—
am I wood or water? Shanks of maple,
hips of seaside roses, he was heaven.
A woman wearing a dress the color of jute.
And woke some more. Mostly fire.
Mostly air. Air was first of all
elements, the movingness before somethingness.
Mornings before a single man has gone to work—
he woke and woke, a few things almost clear.

There is no creator, though a Making Spirit
comes from time to time and welcomes us
from inside out into our own world.
Making things as fast as we can think.
In what language written was the book you never opened?
Who was the mother of the door? Clear too
was the interactive web of influence, a day's your motherfather,
night is your child who dreams you further
into the meek eternity of time. The sun is your little dog.
No wonder kings fear to go to sleep and hate their daughters.
He had been sleeping for a couple of hours
and the sun bit the sea, scorching what sees
until the looking is a kind of dark resentment.
Quiet birds bothered beings he couldn't see.
Desperate loyalists counter rebels in beech woods.
A rabbit hobbles towards the shade.
No religion on an island.
No one will relinquish money, a revolution
is shattering the mirrors only,
doesn't change the endless empire of Light,
every blood-slimed sliver of the glass still reflects
the intolerable injustice of this one-life universe.
He woke and knew it had to be something other,
had to be seed sown in another summer
that we reap here. Or else the meanings
of our mind were only money.
All thought is consolation and an angry man.
He woke late and took a cab to work,
it hurried yellow deep below the bay,
his head hurt with so little sleep,
waking and waking, his whole life an endless
something, carouse, cartouche, his name
held tight in someone's handkerchief, lariat,
the cab crossed the burning plains safe from cheetahs

and reached the northern business district
his eyes were hot with keeping open watching boys
tumbled out and left Russ to pay the fare
with his long Pall Mall cigarettes his failed
midnight. He woke and it was insolent
like any island. Druids came hazarding down
from violet schooners perched in lower clouds
—now under Avalon a wall of sea stones
masoned thick with visionary mortar
held back the lilac thickets still blooming
late as June and the tanager therein
gossiped with the young wife passing
and a duck skims down the sea beach.
Daylight forgives you. Stamina
of sleeping men. It takes
all our energy to stay asleep
when there is so much angry waking.
Into this one bottle he squeezed his vital sap
and woke with a strange feeling in his hands
as if someone held them. Pressure
from inside out. Who wakes?
The house on Canapitsit Neck
looks like a fortress outlined against the levant sun
a small or local gloom, bastille
of energies, all beauty locked in fear. He woke
after three hours sure that someone had died,
a lord or kindly one, sun's serf
perhaps or mind's loving-kindness's minion.
Every time you wake a great king dies.

He woke after four hours with his shirt on inside out
a maiden led him to a fountain or fled him
in the mountains, he drank of whatever he found was flowing,
things come back thirsty from eternity

wake up the day is made of wood
she had to run he slowed to let her hide
smile over shoulder lost in leaves
a grove of aspens quivered by the sea
things he was allowed to remember surely his purpose
to get at the words inside
unfold the greasy red wrappings stained with stars
on our prayer bundle laughing seabirds
fishermen trying to decode the foggy banks
the mind is ultimately happy and all pleasure
comes from its solitude comes from its embrace
he woke reading the coarse grain of granite
smooth insinuations of agate a dimension
washed up on the beach cachinations man or bird
for his embrace the polyester multitudes
Nepali boys strutting by the monastery gates
unsmokably damp cigarettes in monsoons
a breath of hill air and a deep drag to breathe
baseball cap with fishy visor costumes
of the self-dissuaded. It is two hundred
years from the Vendée and finally he gets it.
No one ever wins. It is a process of tossing out the door,
all of us used clothes worn down and cast away
chaff and draff and urinas to build
some Other Body strong and we go out.
Who is the Body all our deaths are buying,
rebel and royalist alike, our black, your white?
He woke after five hours, were they the tops
of fence posts out the window or ancient
monuments up the glacial hill, tips of them
blunt on the far slope face the open sea
the world came from to be here
to meet him. Is he a bird again,
what kind, where is the book he woke?

He heard a tree fall two hundred miles away
it was his heart linden his folk tree his appetite.
Where the giant kept his feelings.
How the wood weeps, how the wind gets in our clothes.
Now things were cooler in him, Egypt further,
deciding against sun glare he knew the fish were there
the ones he wanted, ordered pairs, gods
obscure or youthful powers, knew were there
because he's seen the likes of them
slammed down on jetties gape-mouthed
dead in the quivering air thirty pounds each of them
and a knife in the harbormaster's hand.
Explain the imbrication of their scales, the feint
of color as the sun explored their dying.
Wants to have them in his childhood way,
haddock stew or fried cod, what could be better,
scour the unsuspecting elements for wise animals
not wise to you and eat them. For Wisdom's alkali,
shriek of potassium in dying cells,
if he could sleep long enough he'd understand
the total genome of every species,
the long count. But never why some found it fun to kill.
His hands shook with numbers. Was it numbers?
Inside yourself you sleep alone.
He slept in the toaster in the dinghy in the gap
between two blue rocks on Church's Beach
just before you get to the wild sea poppies
egg yellow in even light he favored.
The smell of freshness in his line-dried shirt
is just another smell. Why choose?
White shoes. A golf cart snarled
and some robins flew away, it's almost sleeping
in him now, shouts of young men
the far-off giggle of island women

at the last end of their slow twilight
mumble in his lips. Patterns.
What could a pattern be but death or sleep?
Glare on pale oak, is he seeing?

He had been sleeping for six hours the lop-sided sun
bothered the dog in his head, something matters
even if it's not his house. Who is a house?
What is a tree on an island? Whose is the
crown now? Twisted circlet bog-iron from the broads
worn round the head of the Queen of the Aurora
in the house of the Sixth Wisdom. Measure him,
he sprawls from hour to hour like a horn.
Or a heron. Or a horse leaps a ditch a spaniel scratches
he lifts time to his teeth and gnaws, he falls
and goes nowhere. There is a settling of accounts
and then there is the quiet water of after.
When nobody is anywhere but where he is
outstretched in shady business
pavilions noisy with bright kept birds, a boy
doing something to a bench. A coat hanger
wakes him. There are rooms up three flights
where after the bars close they took him
to go on drinking, sour red vino in thick coffee cups
and ugly women blaming this and that. Dawn
had nothing to do that day, the wine
was evil but it worked, it almost worked,
there still were bridges over rivers, still rivers, still
subways, the wine couldn't get rid of that—
though it made blurry ruin of what was there
it still was there. Wine ages the world
and makes men young, that is the difference.
Suppose he lived all year on the island,
suppose there were dances in the hedge,

snakeskin left on your doorsill, not war,
just one other visitor, an arrow
prodding gently from behind. The flow of time.
Gypsy gull, sodden dance in mist drench but a dance,
or all the fine high hours when the wind makes up
for the amateur musicians, flugelhorn and clarinet,
sea-bird klezmer, lunatics prancing in the surf
and you can see nothing but the wind. Behavior.
He could at any moment have stopped and just asked
Teach me there is so much I don't know, how could I,
what is my body for and how can I give it to you, explain
how it is to be me coming towards you or you
towards whom I come. Teach me what love meant
by making me. Explain the dirt of feeling
and how to wash, in what surf rinse me clean?
Or is the salt itself the fear, the long contaminant?
Explain fear. But he didn't stop and never asked.
His sleep was bluejay and a broken bottle,
his sleep was beach and stones pressed in him,
discomfort one grows used to, pain
is always new. He woke after seven hours
with the horn blowing, the one he had been bending,
forming out of sheet metal all night long,
some alloy of copper and Miriam, an Egyptian
transit, his arms wet to the elbows turned white.
He folded it and formed it and brazed the seam shut
along the ever-widening smooth trumpet bell-mouth
the slope called history. Full seven hours long it was
and his skin was white as the sound it made
when he pressed it to his lips and instead of
blowing somehow sobbed a mouth of air in
as if we could live on colors alone. What disease
is this now, he thought in waking,
the heron had just gone and nothing is seen of its shadow

for this trumpet was only for the righteous,
like a nun facing out to sea, the wind
plastering her clothes against her inescapable form
or a log burning in the fire or a kingfisher diving,
we can't get away from it, everyone doing what they do.
Around him the theologians jabbered, small
voiced men with big bodies, godding everything
or nothing, anarchs of the ordinary, connoisseurs
of disobedience, a house they said on stilts.
That was his childhood talking. Knives and peach trees,
fishing villages, the boats moored to the pilings
underneath the pretty shacks dove-grey from weather
all opalescent was the salt wood at evening
when he'd wake from his debauch and consult the sea.

For seven hours he had been sleeping
there are secret places in the earth
and all his science was about them
here and there a hill or vista, concrete
pillbox left from her father's war.
She showed him where they had been keeping.
Candles burned below the ground and a goat
bleated at midnight no one could find.
When you stumble onto such a place
you are at once more there
than you have ever felt and touching this
touch all such places. Geopoetry, she guessed,
we make earth. He witnesses. He fears
losing the hour, the Good Hour a friend called
happiness, finding yourself in time and place
and a work fit to your hands
and your hands can skill. Bonheur. The goat
was the wind, olive was aspen, the fallen pillars
sprawled like Carthage and a rabbit sat. Nibble me

also was his mind. Provoke an ecstasy
that convulses all my botany. Use all my words
and rinse me out. He loved that word a life before
sound of water squeezing in his hands to sluice
the dishes clean. The good hour is a rinsing and a step.
At any moment fog will take the mainland
low wind on his wrist, stairs to climb,
messages from Portugal. All my life I told them
how beautiful they are now they must whisper that I am.
A stern stem. Robin transfixed with sunray,
dawns. All the journalists hid beneath the bottles
the rebel colonel snored in the cathedral, his doze
ennobled by flickering blue lights. A church
is always underground. And in mid-air at once.
Foss the cat fell down in fits. The shore of Naxos
shimmered in this nuisance of a mist.
Young mothers whimpered at their cribs. Baby sun,
baby sun, rise in haze and marry me.
The lovely is it way a jackal is concerned
with nothing but his prey. Learn single-mindedness.
And kill—is that the lesson? He thought it was *listening*
but now when the grocer was slicing the roast beef
and the joiner from the mainland lights a dry cigar?
And a grackle sails in? And the deer on the hill
look weird, like things from Australia?
Socrates was of course the end of something, not the start.
Taught in a public way, and taught the young.
Those changes entrained the curious system we endure,
examining the obvious. Should we not teach instead
those who know everything except that one small thing
we ourselves have guessed or figured out or felt?
And shouldn't we do it in the dark? Dream
is the most elite of all academies
and I have spent my science and my poetry

to make it less so, come to me,
hear me, Dream Work, democrat.

He woke after eight hours eating a piece of bread,
a coloring book of little birds, Broad Channel with the herons,
fluting marsh grass in green evening light, a duck,
isn't that enough, a knife? Some weather
is coming, a night is long enough to change the world.
He was shy with her, hopeless (happy) to declare
his needs (not needs) a fairy godmother
laid on him in the cradle such peculiar desires
a great year and a day and a book a cave
a sea a wind even this glaucous lovely mist
would never be morning enough to satisfy.
Curse of guessing who he is
from what he wants. Who wants? All the witches
of Nantucket scream a gentle wind across the sound, stirs
his thinking, how we get in each other's heads,
I feel her thinking. A witch wants him to admire,
her only passion is such admiration. Chilly father I guess,
internalize the enemy, betray your friends.
Dreams are scattered pages of biography,
nobody's life, a book on fire, house clear under water,
horse hurrying in the air, a luminous translucent earth.
Let stand what dream decided. The tigers of Bagdogra
long since awakened to their danger and decamped.
It is what they found along the way that mattered
to most of them, forgetting wontedly why
why were they travelling and to what unlikely goal
they dawdled so beautifully by the shallow river
in soft clothes faded mulberry, pistachio, rainwater white.
Earth watched them with her single eye.
Sharing a little ocean tour he woke and woke
with whaler clamoring and busy fishermen and Spain

cold tips to his fingers he touched himself
counted his ribs, the preliminary weather of the world
was adequate, save him from the adequate
he woke with Persian carpets speaking to him flower by flower
woke with an auctioneer selling him cheap
to the woman in back with straw market basket
couldn't see her face felt her red fingers test his thigh
he woke with a face in his head but whose,
woke with a language he didn't understand
when people spoke at normal tempo to each other,
what are they saying is it to him, woke with the light
confusing him with shadows, woke in an island,
woke with a red ball in his hands he had followed,
man waking in an island, seaplane landing.

Cuttyhunk Island 1993

Holy Sonnets

The thing I am that is not me . . .

Thankmeal our grace is given
Back-pats glib to bless a benefactor
Built before the world, a "lamb"
He said, with intelligent eyes
A devious metaphor, a man who died
Then stopped being dead, a rise
In the rhythm of the mind, come clear.
I wish I could. There is only heart,
Heart and blue women in the street
Whose feet move centimeters above the stone.
Only I mean one heart I mean, a thought
Nestled in the chambers of its care
Different from I am. You want simple?
There is a light that nothing knows.

•

Be like him by being holy not being,
Loopy with definitions and divining,
Smart voices of the local gods emerging
From the sensuous lips of smug channelers
Claiming strange earthrights. A ploy
In lust's legislature, to listen

To her plummy voice inside your private
Arts, bones, preachments, halogens
Whizzing kidneyed to dispose.
You love to listen and not hear.
From the hidden world the information flows
Turns this minute into memory, grants
Last rites and dubious testaments of self.
A myth can only happen to a me.

•

Be glad to god again as if you care
Against all the scary pleurisies of breath
That keep us to our selves, our sodden selves
Taste-worn wintry cabbages dumped
From the noisy squats of rich society.
Be glad to god again as if bright is
And all the thick of you distended
Like a swarm of bees abandoning a tree
You are, still selfless stuffed with honey
For me and for me to exact infinity
From the clumsy calculus of time (one
Pebble after another until none)
Be glad to god again to differentiate
This this from that one and no one sleeps.

•

The diminished responsibility of kings
(The man I am) the watershed deciding
All that has fallen and will fall. Picture
A woods almost unpaved by autumn and the sun
Comes through it rising a fierce clear saying
I am dazed to understand. Mourn

The unmarrying. Love gave me
Some sense of you then let you know me.
Anxiety makes a noise like a string quartet
Rehearsing in my ribcage. Not sleeping well
Night fears flicker through gaunt imagery
Like birds too quick to recognize. The land
I have been given I must rule in my wet way
Like ink seeping into paper to be news.

•

Light through the window of the old barn
With crumpled roof and gaping door and twenty years
It sits in my backyard and I have never entered.
There are things that long to go on pilgrimage
And things that sleep, and weather-beaten structures
Lie thick shrouded in the light itself.
Untamable closeness of things
Where touch is no remedy for ignorance!
Who puts his house here? Old postcards
Show the town with shutters and lawn statues
—Portia rebuking prejudice, Miranda coping with the new—
And deer come homesteading in unseen gardens.
Behind the dozened panes of windows
Nobody I ever knew listened to no music.

•

Have I turned, and what is it to turn?
The body sasses back its boss my aching mind—
Who chases it around the desk, clerk-typist
In an eternally dismal cartoon. Blond body
Of my beast, somber mind of the oldest people,
The clouds roll in on your dumb dialogue.

We get dressed and go home to our wives,
Whatever that is, I stare at a black pen
A doughnut two clean milk bottles—one quart
One pint—a nuthatch upside down on seed.
Nothing must be happening if I am free to annotate
The picturesque vacancy of local mind.
I am frightened of my secretary—
I cannot claim this body that I am.

·

Imagine it against the light and your morning
Work is done. Imagine the light seep through it
And through you vespering, and evening has.
The day was good, the good was given the gift
Out of mind. Serenity of no transaction,
Only knowing and nothing known. For thee
Dear Mind that looks at me my own
From the friend's eyes. Who shows to know.
Time is the answer. The lonely body
In a sea of flesh is one part question
And one part house on fire in the first cartoon—
The deer watch in horror what streaks past
Scorched by imaginary flames. Escape
in my white cart. All thingliness is fugitive.

·

A woman with leaf shimmer on herself
A rubble of light descending makes her visible
And I suppose her too to be my mother and a tree.
For all distractions had broken in the night
(Not vanished) and all materials renew
Their properties in the furnace of desire.

Until wanting is philosophy enough. End
Of the road. Time for time again. Orders
To fill. Destinies in a cracked shell. Dawn.
What has to be done is milk this lovely fire.
Give yours away. Let theirs become you
Till you look in the mirror and see only them,
The years have paid your toll for you, go now,
Break into small shivers of light that know me.

•

Knocked down by omens the ticket brokers
Reassign your seat. Under the eagle
Not the bust of Verdi. The overture
Has been playing forever and the curtain
Seems to be trembling but it might be your eyes.
Outside, snow is falling on the postcards
Drowsy flower girls in chubby doorways
And lonely long black cars. Will you understand
It when it does begin? Or be distracted
By the beauty of the people up there so pink
Wandering around in light? Will the tunes
Take you to that all too private place
You came here to leave back home?
Close your eyes in case you're all alone.

•

And if they did not listen would I not speak
Freer and more suitorly, sweeting the sun up
As if I could and heal the fire hides in grease
To warm your hands so—by that—suddenly you know
Someone is speaking? From the heat in your hands
From the moon on your fingernail, tell, tell.

Until there is all telling and nothing told.
Then you are the story, and cast no shadow.
Short of breath you still catch up with the light.
But they are listening. I thought the myths
Were all inside but when I speak you hear them,
My obvious mistake. Out it, out
With the holy business, heart scraps and hopes,
I wrestled with your enemies till I was one.

•

The fur of things be kind or animal
I need a morning of not going.
I call myself by the name the mountain needs
—We are identitied by place—
By fur in sunlight by a fallen tree
You can rest on and watch the river
—Wind can only talk when someone listens
Did you think she was a babbler
This animal of touch? The storm
Is a jade stone and falls from the sky
Earth is the mirror that it breaks
We are the luck—some good some rough—
That last as long as we can see
Thousands of half-moons in a stormy lake.

•

All night the clouds wait to be let out: he
Went into the Dark Factory and unpieced them there,
Densed mist into hard frost and this he fused
To waking emptiness by dint of dawn: sun now
In a cloudless sky. If no sheep, no need to shepherd
Them to winter valleys and to summer alps,

No need for wolves. If no clouds, no words need
Describe. Free we move, shadow-makers
Making shadows in the sun. Turn us transparent
And the work is done. The evaporation.
Trade it all for salt and throw the salt into the sky.
Usually ending is the hardest time but here
Wind closes our work for us, endlessly giving,
Slamming the door on an empty room.

The Door

I.

Then there was the waiting
on the other side of the door
waiting for you
because the wood of the door
said your name

when I looked very close
saw you and your name
wreathed or writhed together
like the shadow of smoke
easing from a candle tip
when the wind has made
free of the light

first of all
we are citizens of things

and then you answered
I heard the sounds
inside the room
(the room is what a door
is trying to say)

there was a movement
and that was you

coming forward
lightfooted as a crow
to open the door
I hoped or just stand
near it with your cheek
pressed against the wood
hearing me breathe
on the other side of the world.

2.

Because they were waiting
there is a word

a door

how many woods have you been made from
how many ships carried you here

never and no one I am a door

I am the door
and the clock had something to say and the wall
and the cat lay on the windowsill in sunshine

forever
because in a door nothing is different

open or closed a door stays

you think: it is the house that hurries
now and the sky
pours down over the horizon
tired of carrying all that staying

suddenly gushed

or you think: I will get up from this chair
and carry a light bulb into a dark room
and wonder why I have come there

and the door knows

I am the door he said
but didn't tell us how to listen
we know how to listen to a bird to a train passing
two hundred cars of it heading south full of silage and glue
we know how to listen to a river

but a door creaks or slams you can listen to that
but you think: no, that is what someone does to a door
that's listening to people again or listening to houses

the house is running so fast now
we will never catch it
it is full of ourselves overweight and drinking lime kool-aid
listening to the war
there was always a war then and the sun went in and out
and that was before the peach pit
flung to the asphalt rebounded
and smote the afreet's grandchild on the eye

that was before the hopscotch diagram drowned under blood
you still see the white lines a little

the brave straight lines meeting at angles
sharp as the edge of a door

you think: my mother was the lintel my father was the post
you think: the door is a much kinder mirror
you think: no matter how far there's always a door before me
you think: I will be an admiral of doorways
you think: there is no stopping me

the kingdom of heaven is like a lock on no door
a door with no wall
a wall with no house
a house in the air

you think: there is always someplace to go

                out and out or in and in or both together
                like an old song from an empty country
                only the crow on the dead tree remembers
the crow creaks like a door in the sky

you think: there may be no place to go

in and out the doorknob under your fingers
the sway of the great harp of it
swinging on its hinges
you plunge it in and out of its doorhole
swinging it in and out like a great concertina
the air rushes this way and that way
the papers rise from the table and flutter, this is the news

you think: that is only something to do with a door
                but what is a door

I am the door he said *through me* he said
there is some kind of going
you think: I will go through the door
but the door goes with you.

3.

But what is made from
the door

from wool or from wheat
or both together

was it an animal
who left it there alone
like a tuft of tawny fur
stuck to a thorn bush
or like a scat of its droppings
steaming in the autumn chill

is it like a pool of milk in the goat yard
spilled when a nanny shifted the way they do
and the girl who takes care of the goats
missed a beat on the downpull
and the teat gushed ivory onto the chaffy ground

what tree does it come from
and how does a tree do it
the rigid rightness of things
without contrivance standing into the sky

I am the door and I am made by myself
you can open me and close me

or lean against me at twilight
listening to the finches bicker among seed hulls

what is it made from, this door that is there
you think: it is there forever
it must be made from nothing but itself

but it has no self it is a door only a door
opening and closing and not about anything

I am the door he said I have no self, I am not about anything

you came back from a far country and it was waiting
and wherever you traveled it was ahead of you
waiting at the end of every day
a hard dog, a sunset built out of wood

it is all the roads in the world all at once

but what is it made from, this door
you think, or any door
why can't I put my hand on its matter
its elemental its essence
the way I can put my hand on its doorknob
or rest my scratchy cheek against its panes
whispering the name of my wife
so that only the door can hear it
open open to her
the way all my life the door has seemed to obey me

bringing me deeper into room after room of my life

and it was always the same door wasn't it

you think: the door is made of habits or of nothing
you think: the door is made of going through
you think: the door is made of me

but there is always something there that isn't you
something that reminds you of a tree
yes, something growing not too far from anybody
something hard and useful and answerable when you ask
yes, but something that isn't that either
something no kinder than glass something
emptier than steel, a crystal
with nobody home a broken radio a child's thumbprint
left on the window of a closed store

what is it made from this door nobody knows
you think: someone I love
standing in the doorway
tells me all I need to know about doors

but beyond anything you know how to know
the door sways open and open its powerful wing.

Devotions and Permissions:
Some notes on these selected poems

The Alchemist. When I finished writing this poem (halfway to dawn, Brooklyn), it seemed the first full poem I had written. It crossed some line that made me me. I had the nerve to dedicate it to Robert Duncan, with reverence. The strange riddling chilly love duet between Calaf and Turandot in Puccini's opera is worked with through the poem.

Hui-neng Chops Bamboo. The celebrated ink painting of the Zen patriarch. I couldn't stop looking at it. After a time, it made me think that all marks anywhere are inscription, all signs are writing.

The Exchanges. The early sections of this long poem had at first the title *Spiritum*, and appeared in my first book. A year later (1962) the whole poem came out in *Origin*, well-guided by Cid Corman. The poem, begun in 1959, owes a lot to early readings in Levi-Strauss (*Tristes tropiques* has just been published as *World on the Wane*), Curtius, and Erich Auerbach.

An Epitaph. Originally meant to honor the memory of Edwin Muir.

Lectiones. The title of a series of "readings," experiments with the boundaries between prose and verse, towards quicker or more intense modes of discourse.

An *haruspex* is the augur who interprets the outer and inner flight of birds.

"Face in the rock wall" was dedicated to Laura Furman.

Lunes. For years I had loved what I knew, heard, guessed of haiku, especially as revealed in that wonderful old four volume set, one for each season, by the Zen/Tennysonian R.H. Blyth. But all the English haiku I found or tried to write seemed flabby or slack. Maybe seventeen were too many syllables for English, which is much more monosyllabic than Japanese. I tried trimming, and got finally to a five-three-five pattern, concave rather than convex, thirteen syllables, number of the lunar months. I called the form a lune, and wrote many. In older English, lunes also means madness.

Up on Autumn. A fantasia on themes of ancient musical instruments— lyre from cowhorns, lute from turtle shell—autumn as death time and New Year, Rosh ha-Shana. The poem is pervaded with acrostical play on schoolchild's mnemonics for the spaces and lines of the musical staves. It was written for my friend Marvin Gelfand, economist, hence Adam and Adam Smith, whose wife May Ebihara gave birth to their first son Adam in the week his father died. Joining those ceremonies is my own grandfather Thomas Kane who died the day I was born—my aunts did not tell my mother her father was dead for fear she would lose her milk. Music from such pain rears up ever.

State of the Nation. Meditates using images and text from Titania's exalted complaint to Oberon about human anguish and its "natural" occasions, in *A Midsummer Night's Dream*. A Ngaio Marsh detective novel set among folk dancers and mummers gets brought into play too. It is dedicated to Robert Duncan, with variations on the severe chant of the presidents in his Pindar poem.

Devotions XVIII—The Wood Man. In the first edition, the Greek text was printed in Greek characters, absurd thing to do but I still want the sound of it IN the lines, so I've put the meaning of the lines at the end, and transliterated the sound of the ancient Greek, assuming that phi (for example) represents p+aspiration, rather than an f sound. So p', k' and t' instead of ph-, ch- and th-.

Axon Dendron Tree. A long poem organized on a numeric structure. Each section consists of III unnumbered stanzas; the first section's stanzas are of nine lines each, the second section's of eight, and so on, diminishing to the last section, 111 one-line stanzas. In my own sense of my work, this is my first real achievement using any sort of compositional grid or organizing principle other than the Local Music, which has always been the self-arising guide of the poem.

The few passages here are from the section of Fives, excerpts which meditate on kingship—King Ædwin's sparrow, King Agamemnon's murder, and the child-king here unnamed of Isis and Osiris whom the Egyptians called Horus.

The whole poem is dedicated to Louis Zukofsky, in thanks for his creative kindness, as a poet to us all, and as a man to me when I was beginning. He is one of the Four Masters (with Olson, Duncan, Blackburn) who boxed my ears.

"Salitter" is a word from alchemy used by Jakob Boehme for a certain vivid potency of God.

Alpha. A sequence originally dedicated to Timotha Doane.

Stanzas from Dante. A homeophonic translation of the great hymn to the Virgin Mary that Dante gives Saint Bernard of Clairvaux to sing at the end of the *Paradise.*

The Death of Rasputin. A poem simply recording the traditional accounts of the death of the so-called monk. It must be said that for some reason Rasputin was my father's favorite term of endearment for me when I was a child; it was many years before I learned what manner of man my prototype was—if we even know now.

Alba. A dawn song. Krakatoa is the Indonesian volcano, now and properly spelled Krakatao, but they called it -oa, when I was in school. The ashes from its eruption darkened the world in the Nineteenth Century—and made the sad "year with no summer."

Last Light. Feather-horned Venus is Quetzalcoatl. This is America, after all.

Sonnet 18. Le Pendu is The Hanged Man, as in the Tarot card. The poet Nerval is said to have hanged himself in the middle of a winter night, outdoors, with no shelter. His reasons are not known. He becomes here the type of all willing self-sacrificers, wise or foolish, Odin on his tree, all those who darken themselves to make something come, wisdom, or help for others, or blank surcease.

Song XXI. The landscape is Boston and the whole plain along the Charles, as seen from the hill in Roxbury. A view from a hill, the whole world seen. The Nile and the River Charles intertwine. (All of Songs I–XXX speculate Egypt.)

The 18th Trump is the Moon card in the Tarot, stirrings from the unconscious, something this way comes.

Ashera is the fertility deity of Canaan, whose name the Hebrews interspersed with the vowels of *bosheth*, "shame," to arrive at the name Ashtoreth. Or so they used to explain the name given to great Astarte in the Judean hills. Ashera was said to have been represented by, and worshipped as, an upright unbranched sapling—perhaps not unlike the original wooden tree or stump called the Palladium, the most sacred of Athenian hallows.

Kane's mark. My mother's maiden name was Kane. She inherited from her father Thomas and passed on to me a raised plumy left eyebrow traditional in the family. It used to strike people as a devilish sign, and my mother used to keep trying, in vain, to train it down (on her brow and on mine). We lived among Italians, and I sometimes got the ancient sign from old women—index finger and pinky out, other fingers in: the bull skull of ancient Crete, the horns, which meant to ward off evil long before it meant to mock a cuckold. No wonder that like a baby from Byron I confused this mark with the mark (also on the forehead) of Cain, Cain Adamson, the first bane.

Aither. The Greeks had two levels in their sky: *aither* was the high bright changeless world the Gods knew, and that we now travel through with composure in jets, looking out above all the clouds at the gold and blue. *Metarsia* was the weather down here. We have that too.

Injune. Pelagius was the Welsh or Irish theologian (his name, "Of the Sea," might indicate an original name like Morgan) who lived around the year 400. His teachings seemed to deny original sin, and to recognize impermanence and death as a natural and inevitable part of existence, rather than a punishment for lapse. A much greater emphasis inevitably has to be laid on human act rather than on divine command or divine grace. It is easy to imagine the Britain of King Arthur and the Grail legends as having been formed by a Pelagian drift of piety.

William Mount, the Luminist. I'm thinking of that famous canvas, "Eel Fishing near Setauket." The heralding light arriving, the evening sheen of water. No one has shown me better that Long Island light, all human and lagoony. But Essex and Apple are at the end of Cape Anne, the furthest reach of the glacial moraine of which Long Island, the Elizabeths, and Cape Cod are largely formed. Among the painted and the actual woods and waters of America, the mysteries of the Freemasons are never far. "The Masses, the masses!" is the title and full text of a choral song by Charles Ives.

Mudra. The shape is the vesica piscis of art history, the "fish-bladder" shape—the shape formed by the overlapping of two circles whose circumferences touch each other's center. It was long enough regarded as a feminine symbol to become the standard heraldic shape on which to display a woman's armorial bearings.

A Fable. Depends on Apuleius's great story of Cupid and Psyche, the central interpolated narrative in his *Metamorphoses* (usually called *The Golden Ass*).

The Book of the Running Woman. The biblical Abraham/Hagar/Ishmael story quickened by the koranic continuation of the story of Hagar (her name must be from the same Semitic root as *hegira*— Mohammed's flight to Medinah, by which Muslims still reckon the years) and her banishment with her son Ishmael, and her flight through the deserts to southern Arabia. The well is Zam-Zam, still a sacred site during the Pilgrimage. The poem was my first awkward attempt to understand and adore the figure of woman fleeing utterly from the patriarchal into her own order. It is her blessing that makes the desert rock give water. The single mother whose child becomes father of the Arabs. *Scheidekunst* is the older German for "alchemy," literally the art of separation; the word looks however like the art of the sheathe, or as if it meant the vaginal art.

An die ferne Geliebte. The title, "to the distant beloved," of a Beethoven song cycle I listened to many times—oh the ways we learn distance!

Ea, Enki and Enlil are Sumerian gods; their provinces are made clear in the poem.

Williams is William Carlos Williams.

A Constant Telling of the Father and His Widdershins. Widdershins means literally "against the sun," i.e., west to east or counter-clockwise, the way witches were thought to dance around a church in order to combat the holy. I pretend the word means against-Sons, the contradictory children. They fight for their freedom—the chance to move. Widdershins contrasts with Deosil, sunwise, east to west.

Elgar's Second Symphony. Dedicated to Jonathan Williams.

The Sound. Dedicated, all too late, to the poet April Hubinger, who once wrote an essay on the poem that told me more than I had known.

In Mahler's Sleep. Dedicated to the poet Jonathan Williams, thanks to our shared passion for Mahler's music. The section beginning "By the stream almost dark now" was set to music by Peter Garland.

Linguistics. Using a slightly earlier version of this sequence, the composer Bruce Wolosoff composed a song cycle for mezzo-soprano and chamber ensemble (flute, bass clarinet, violin, cello and piano). I have not yet heard it performed.

Mihrab. A niche in the wall of the mosque indicating the direction of Mecca, towards which one directs prayers.

Love Song 1. I had been invited to watch the running of the grunion, small fish who in uncountable phosphorescent multitudes arrive on the beaches of San Diego one night of the year.

The Loom. Raymond Lull is Ramon Llul, the Catalan mage, who seems to have thought brilliantly, and guessed that if we must have art, let it be the art of knowing.

The Sonata in A flat is Beethoven's next to last piano sonata, the thirty-first. Its *arioso dolente* [a mournful songlike thing] is a brief and poignant melody that arises in the midst of a profound research of means, measures, beginnings, silences. The sonata ends with a great double fugue, by which the poem is driven.

Ode 15. Delos is the ancient island sanctuary of truce and diplomacy, hope of the Greek commonwealth. Negus is an old word for an Ethiopian potentate. (Not the posset.)

The Tears of Edmund Burke. Drawn from the article on Burke by Viscount Morley in the Eleventh Edition of the *Encyclopaedia Britannica*. It dwells, with a fervor rare in reference books, on the intensity of Burke's personal feelings for the slain queen, Marie Antoinette.

Chastity. Stavros, stauros, Greek word for the cross.

An Acquisition. From a large beautifully formed spiderweb I saw in Muir Woods, California, among the redwood and Oregon laurel.

Les Joueurs de Foot-Ball. My father's brother Seymour, who called himself my Uncle Simon, and was the only man I ever knew who still used thee and thou, lived years as an invalid after being poison-gassed in the Great War.

The Book of Persephone. Plutone is Pluto/Hades/Aides, the lord of the Underworld, who abducted Persephone. The king is here heard as the basso profundissimo who sings the role of the dark patriarch in Monteverdi's *Ballo dell' Ingrate*.

Studies from the Mishnah. DBR = dalet bet resh, the triliteral root from which words for speaking come, and also the word for "thing."

Early Spring Day Along the Housatonic. Dedicated to John Ashbery.

Sentence. The poem is the furthest reach I got to in my experiments with polysyntax—which I understand as the permission to take any or every word or phrase as linkable with what comes before, or with what comes after, or as capable of bearing meaning while standing alone. So any continuous text is in fact rife with moves, forward, backward, stopping and recovering—syntax reaches as far as our lust for meaning lets it. And that's the joy of it.

Cathedral of the Incarnation. Small and elegant, built by the money of the Scottish-American department store king Alexander Stewart, it stands up from the Salisbury Plain—the great flat interior of Long Island now occupied by Hempstead.

Gethsemani. The garden in which Jesus underwent that foreseeing of his passion called, traditionally, the Agony in the Garden, and where he for a moment seemed to wish the cup to pass untasted.

Spring Sonnet. Dedicated to Harry Mathews.

When the brokers were raining on Wall Street. Dedicated to my mother, Margaret Kane Kelly, 1902–1990.

Postcards from the Underworld. From a sequence originally dedicated to Lisa Katzman.

The Head of Orpheus. This, the first rhymed poem I had written in thirty years, was set to music by Nicholas Maw.

Variations on a Poem of Stefan George. I got started with a casual, literal translation of George's German poem; that entrained a series of variations that gradually but inexorably turned homeophonic (a poetry of "sounds-like," trying to hear another language as one's own), and led at last to the final variation, which was the German original itself.

A Stone Wall in Providence. Dedicated to Mary Caponegro, who lived across from the wall that keeps the sports of Brown unseen from who knows what travellers on Angell Street, safe from people walking big dogs down Arlington.

Dampier's Voyages. Suggested by some passages in the journals of William Dampier, mariner.

The Man Who Loved White Chocolate. There is a touch of autopsycho-biography about this poem that does not please me, and I have to keep confessing, though I like the poem well enough to keep doing so.

Towards the Day of Liberation. Written as a birthday poem for George Quasha, born on Bastille Day, 14 July.

Elegy. Dedicated respectfully to John Hawkes, who liked it, and told me tears came into his eyes as he read the last lines—may every text have such a reader!

Melencolia. So spelled from the engraving by Albrecht Dürer that shows a pensive Wisdom seated on and amidst philosophical instruments of analysis and demonstration. Far from meaning sadness, it means the exaltation of Saturn—all the arts of measurement, along with probity, longevity, clarity—in Libra—art, beauty, serenity. The poem is dedicated to Lydia Davis.

A Flower for the New Year. The Smiths are Sidney Smith of St Catharine's and his sister Kate. He was the editor of Darwin's papers.

Afterdeath. Within nine months I lost to death my friend Mary Moore Goodlett (1950–1990) in January, my mother in August, my father (Samuel Jason Kelly, 1900–1990) in September. I was present at the moment of death of the friend and the father. Who can watch his mother die? I kept trying to understand, and there is so little to.

Ariadne. The passages here are the first third of the poem. It was dedicated with love and excitement to Charlotte Mandell, who is now my wife.

The themes involve centuries of Ariadne, who loved a man and was betrayed, who loved a God and was fulfilled. Exile and dwindling conviction of one's worth. Homer speaks, his ears full of his own music—what teaches us to hear has deafened him, is that it?

An opera takes place in the middle, modeled plainly but vaguely on Richard Strauss's *Ariadne on the Island of Naxos*, an opera about an opera inside a play inside a story, an interweaving of bourgeois and heroic. I pretend that Ariadne, the name, is Semitic, and derives from some such form as **ari ad' nah*, Our Lady the Lion.

Prince Andrei Looks at the Sky. The famous moment in *War and Peace*, when the prince, suddenly wounded, lies on the ground and sees what we never let ourselves see. The delirium in italics is a homeophonic translation of Tolstoy's description of the scene in Russian.

Set on War. The horrid little Gulf War was getting started, and its timing was frightening: the fifteenth of January 1991 was the deadline of the ultimatum given by the Western Aggressors to the Midden Eastern Aggressors. We are still dying from that full-scale short-attention-span war.

 Penikese Island is a tiny island in Buzzards Bay, ten miles or so off New Bedford in Massachusetts, which was used as a leper colony for many years. The graves of the lepers are still intact.

Reading Li Shang-yin. The poem is a meditation reading through the first six lines of an eight-line poem by the T'ang poet Li Shang-yin. The translation is by Lisa Raphals, who sent it to me. The words in italics in the poem, taken in order, constitute her translation of Li's lines.

Patmos. Dedicated to Pierre Joris and Nicole Peyrafitte, in whose house in Encinitas it was written. Patmos is the island where St John the Evangelist in old age wrote the *Apocalypse* (or *Book of Revelations*), and it is also the mind's island Hölderlin visited in his great hymn. I was at the time working vainly on a homeophonic translation of that hymn.

Mapping. A cluster of circumstances around survey maps given me by Christina Coyle, a lunch with Roger Deutsch and Nisse Hope, Nisse doodling, a drive with Pat and Marla Smith to an Indian restaurant in the Taconics, passing through the scene of a violent crime, Marla talking about birds. Of any such terrain a map tries to make sense.

[*AH*] is how the Tibetan character, last in their alphabet, is pronounced.

The Phantom of the Opera. The epigrams at the top of each section are taken from the screen titles in Rupert Julian's epochal film visualization (ca. 1928) of Gaston Leroux's novel. This poem is dedicated to that neglected New Zealand director and that intricate French romancier.

Satyr Mourning a Nymph. The poem says where and how the poem is. I wish we could all wake up late on a rainy London morning and stroll over to have a look at it.

Bartholomew *Gosnold* was an acquaintance of William Shakespeare; he did some acting and some exploring in the early 1600s. On one voyage he settled some of his crew on Cuttyhunk Island (westernmost of the Elizabeths, off the elbow of Cape Cod). They lasted one winter, and seem to have been the earliest English settlers in the present United States.

Voyage to the Center of the Earth. The title is from Jules Verne's Icelandic adventure, the descent into the Snæfells volcano.

The Triads. The name must suggest the ancient Triads of the Island of Britain (see Rachel Bromwich's great study), though the poem takes from them only the threefoldness of argument—a line against a line answered by a line. *Scamander* was the river of Troy. *Corbenic* was the strange sacred city to which the Grail knights came at the end of their quest.

Man Sleeping. The places names and circumstances are those of Cuttyhunk Island, between the mainland and Martha's Vineyard.

In 1980 Jed Rasula edited *The Alchemist to Mercury* (Richard Grossinger, North Atlantic). It is an "alternate" selected poems for 1960–1980, chosen by Rasula from poems that had not appeared in my books. Some are reprinted here, but restored to their original chronological order. Rasula's introduction and selection still guide me.

Printed September 1995 in Santa Barbara
& Ann Arbor for the Black Sparrow Press by
Mackintosh Typography & Edwards Brothers Inc.
Text set in Centaur by Words Worth.
Design by Barbara Martin.
This edition is published in paper wrappers;
there are 200 cloth trade copies;
100 hardcover copies have been numbered & signed
by the author; & there are 26 lettered copies
handbound in boards by Earle Gray, each with
an original holograph poem by the poet.
These holograph poems make up a series called
Postcards from Mnemosyne.

Photo: Charlotte Kelly

ROBERT KELLY lives in upstate New York with his wife, the translator Charlotte Mandell. He has long been associated with the writing program at Bard College, where he continues the practice of his own writing. He has published more than fifty books of poetry and fiction, the latest of which are *Mont Blanc* and *Queen of Terrors* respectively. *Red Actions: Selected Poems 1960–1993* is his most recent publication. In 1994 he was honored with the degree of Doctor of Letters awarded by the State University of New York.